# WHEN
## THE
# SOUTH
## WAS
# SOUTHERN

# Embattled Emblem

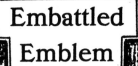

O hated flag, I hold you high
  To shine as beacon light
To all the weak in foreign lands
  Who battle for the right.
For once you waved above our land —
  The South, in all her might —
And gave us cheer when days were drear —
  A widow's lamp by night.

Ah, but that was years ago,
  Cry those who loathe our Cause.
Forget, repent, and cease your praise
  Of men who brought you loss.
Should we despise that loss of life,
  Or even loss of Cause?
Far greater man once took a stand
  That led Him to a cross.

They curse, revile, and burn you
  In perverted zealotry,
While those who feel the despot's heel
  Hymn well your liberty.
O sacred flag, O Rebel flag,
  O battle flag of Lee —
May all my days be filled with praise
  Of Southland, God, and thee!

— Michael Andrew Grissom

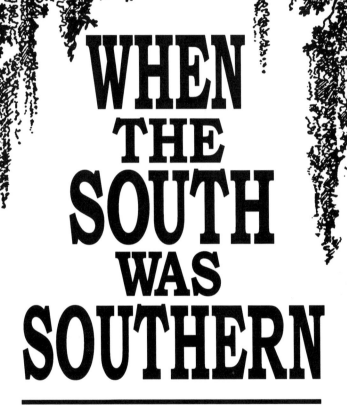

# WHEN THE SOUTH WAS SOUTHERN

### By Michael Andrew Grissom

**PELICAN PUBLISHING COMPANY**
Gretna 1998

First printing, October 1994
Second printing, May 1998

**Library of Congress Cataloging-in-Publication Data**

Grissom, Michael Andrew.
    When the South was Southern / Michael Andrew Grissom.
        p.  cm.
    Includes index.
    ISBN 1-56554-092-1
    1. Southern States—History—Pictorial works. 2. Southern States-
-Social life and customs—Pictorial works.  I. Title.
F210.G78  1994
975'.043'0222—dc20                                              94-5239
                                                                   CIP

Manufactured in the United States of America
Published by Pelican Publishing Company, Inc.
1101 Monroe Street, Gretna, Louisiana 70053

# TABLE OF CONTENTS

Elba R. Grissom

The motivating force in my life has always been my dad. He has always pushed me to greater heights. When a small state college would have sufficed, he urged me to enroll in the University of Oklahoma. When a bachelor's degree seemed sufficient, he encouraged me to get a master's degree. When singing and entertaining around home showed a little promise, Daddy encouraged me to move to Nashville.

Writing was new territory for me — and for Daddy. But when it looked like I wasn't going to be able to find a publisher for my first effort, I got a call from home. It was Daddy. He told me to hang onto that manuscript, that it was a good book, and that someday someone would recognize its worth and publish it. That manuscript became *Southern By the Grace of God*.

When times got rough and I got down, Daddy found the right words to keep me going. At some point, he always looked at me with those understanding eyes and said, "Now, Mike, it's not the end of the world."

In June, the world ended. Ten days after an ill-advised operation, Daddy suddenly died in the early morning hours of June 2. I had left his bedside only minutes before he suffered cardiac arrest and, but for a quirk of fate, would have been there in the final moments.

I guess you might say Daddy and I belonged to a mutual admiration society. He loved everything I wrote, and I loved everything he did. He was my number one fan, and he was the inspiration for all three of my books. I regret that he saw only two pages of this one, for it was only partially complete when I rushed home to see about him.

We didn't clean out Daddy's closet. We didn't throw away his belongings. Everything is still there, just the way he left it. As I straightened up a few things on the little table next to his favorite chair, there lay the three books in which he constantly read: *The Bible, Southern By the Grace of God*, and *The Last Rebel Yell*.

So, to my hero, my inspiration, and the light of my life, I dedicate this book. Daddy, I love you and miss you — and shall as long as life shall last.

# FOREWORD

This volume closes the trilogy of southern culture which began with the release of *Southern By the Grace of God* in the summer of 1988.

For many years, southerners had reeled under the blows of an all-out assault upon our singular way of life — a way that once was definable in clearly drawn lines. No phase of our culture was left unattacked. Everything was game — our ethnic customs, our dialect, our religious beliefs, our social structure, our cherished traditions, our icons, and the symbols of our identity. And yet, for all the slings and arrows, not one single southern author stepped up to bat for our side.

There were southern historians who chugged on, turning out scholarly works on generals, battles, and military operations. We had novelists who never missed a publisher's deadline. And we beheld talented home-grown writers churning out book after book of fabulous folklore garnered from the hills and mountains of the upper South and the bayous of the lower South. But we waited in vain for one of those established southern authors to take pen in hand and defend the dear old South in her days of despair. Even southern born writers in exile were loath to come to the aid of their homeland, choosing instead to pile on, fatuously deluded into thinking one shows his intelligence by denigrating his own background.

Weeks turned into months, months into years, and years into decades, while the average southerner, of whom I am most average, became increasingly frustrated. It was out of sheer desperation, born of this insufferable state of affairs, that I — one who had never written anything worth remembering — finally embarked upon what was intended to be a temporary diversion from my regular occupation. *Southern By the Grace of God* was the result, and it seemed to do what a much more capable writer could have — and should have — done. It reinvigorated a much-maligned group of wonderful people called *southerners!*

By 1990, many southerners were regaining some lost ground in the area of self-image, but it seemed that the overall situation was becoming worse. We saw incessant demands to remove from public view our sacred monuments and symbols. Violence and intimidation increased, and there seemed to be a sort of resignation setting in. In February of 1991, *The Last Rebel Yell* was released in hopes of shoring up our defenses, reassuring those who remained at their posts, and encouraging the intimidated to rejoin the fray.

Southern By the Grace of God was intended to educate the southerner to his neglected past and rebuild his shattered pride. In *The Last Rebel Yell*, the message is amplified to state the traditional southern position and rally our people to assert themselves in defense of the culture. *When the South Was Southern* attempts to round out the whole by presenting visual images of who and what we were, so that our vision of the future is reflective of a clear and highly revered past.

So much of our southernness has given way to the forces of mass media, big government, enforced conformity, and unbridled socialism that modern southerners may be somewhat surprised to learn that southern communities were once more than cookie cutter copies of fast food strips and Burger Kings. A real southern atmosphere prevailed, and it is that aura that this book attempts to convey through the miracle of the camera.

Photography began in 1839 in Paris, France. It was brought to America by Samuel F.B. Morse, developer of the Morse Code. The first images were on pieces of glass and were called daguerreotypes. By 1852, a similar type of image on glass was being produced and called an ambrotype. Daguerreotypes were made between 1839 and 1860, while ambrotypes were in vogue between 1852 and 1880.

In the 1860s, many photographs were developed on sensitized pieces of enameled tin. Called tintypes, these odd little metal photographs were popular through the 1890s. They were cut in many irregular shapes, and the images were usually rather dim and gray-looking without sharp contrasts.

By far the most popular medium was paper. Pictures were developed on photographic paper and glued to pieces of cardboard called studio cards. Known as cabinet prints, they were widely used from 1868 through 1914. A smaller version, measuring approximately 2 3/8" by 4" and in most cases featuring only the head or head and shoulders of a person, was called a *carte de visite* and was used at times as a calling card. The *carte de visite* was popular from 1859 through 1905.

Locating photographs for such an extensive work is a slow, tedious process and must be done in person, all across the South. My own personal collection, which continues to grow, was the primary source, and friends and acquaintances throughout Dixie provided some fascinating specimens through generous loans; but old photographs are increasingly hard to find, and I eventually turned to the vast archival collections of public institutions and private foundations, only to find the cost prohibitive. Deadlines were fast approaching, and the acquisition of historic photographs had slowed to a trickle, leaving me with what appeared to be no solution.

Every cloud must have a silver lining, so they say, and in this case the silver turned out to be the vast world of postcards—not yet gobbled up by museums and archives. Forced to seek photographs elsewhere, I turned to the flea markets and antique malls of the South, discovering the jewels that lay among the endless boxes of old postcards. Here were the quaint old scenes, the highways and byways, and assorted items of interest to southerners during the first half of this century. So rich was the trove that it constitutes a substantial portion of this volume.

*When the South Was Southern,* in its entirety, is a photographic collection of southerners, southern events, and places in the South. At first, it was decided that only pictures pre-dating 1920 would be used, but the '20s and '30s yielded such excellent specimens, especially among the postcards, that exceptions were soon being made. Most of the photographs in this work have never before been published except, of course, in the case of the postcards.

It is fervently hoped that *When the South Was Southern,* the closing volume of this trilogy, will complement the two earlier volumes in such a way that no southerner, after having read them, will ever be at loss to "give an answer to every man that asketh you a reason of the hope that is in you," if I may be so bold as to appropriate the words of the Apostle Peter to this lesser, though dear, cause.

Old photographs need special care. They fade when exposed to the light. Keep them in a box or drawer. Never frame and hang them on the wall. If you want to display an old photograph, have it copied, and frame the copy. Store the original in a dark place. Handle photographs by the edges only. Fingers leave oily prints that damage the image.

# PART ONE

VICKSBURG, MISSISSIPPI, 1885. This busy scene at Vicksburg was a common sight during the decade of the '80s when the steamboat era was at its peak. In the foreground, the *Leflore* is loaded with bales of ginned cotton.

2

TENNESSEE, ca. 1898. Bob Wright.

ARKANSAS, ca. 1890. The South was built upon the backs of hard-working people like this — the rural families of the South. Even though the work was hard and lasted all day, folks like this had too much self-respect to complain and look for a handout. Mama probably read the Bible by the light of a coal oil lamp, and Daddy made sure that no one went hungry. Even though all of the clothes any one of them possessed could be hung on a nail behind the door, come Sunday they would be wearing the best they had to the nearest country church. People were honest, marriages lasted, and the welcome mat was always out. Southerners who spring from such stock have nothing to live down and a lot to live up to.

FANNIN COUNTY, TEXAS, ca. 1895. William Hilliard Burkes, who lived in the Elwood/Telephone area near the Red River.

TENNESSEE, ca. 1908. Addison Beaurat Ford, one of the old soldiers who lived his last years in the Confederate Soldiers Home at *The Hermitage*. He had been a private in Company A, 17th Tennessee Cavalry, and was married to Sallie Pocahontas Bolling. He is shown here proudly wearing the Southern Cross of Honor, given to Confederate veterans by the UDC, who began awarding the medals in 1900. (Courtesy Albert Baxendale, Jr.)

CARROLL COUNTY, VIRGINIA, ca. 1920. A group of loggers who worked the forests around the Virginia-North Carolina state line. (Courtesy Larry Alderman)

HATTIESBURG, MISSISSIPPI, ca. 1895. Two little southern belles in the making. Photographed in Pitts' Studio.

WYNNEWOOD, INDIAN TERRITORY, ca. 1895. It's probably October or early November, and the planters have brought their cotton to town. They have been to the gin, where the cotton was baled, and are now headed with their bales to the Alliance Cotton Yard at the south end of this street — Commercial Avenue. One gin was located on North Commercial, and another was located to the right out on West Main Street. George Hervey Geer, the photographer, came to Wynnewood in1890 and left on Thanksgiving Day, 1896, moving to a farm he had bought sight unseen in Lawrence County, Tennessee.

TULSA, INDIAN TERRITORY, ca. 1900. (Next page) All that is known about this unusual photograph is that it was made by the Hubbert Studio of Tulsa. Notice that all of the men are holding what appears to be advertisements for a shoe company. One even has them stuffed in his boots. Was this perhaps a group of well-known people — maybe entertainers — who are endorsing a particular brand of footwear? The picture appears to have been taken on a stage somewhere, and the presence of the young boy and the little girl indicate that this may have been a popular family act.

SOUTH CAROLINA, ca. 1861. Pvt. Albert Stone, a Confederate soldier in Wade Hampton's Legion, Longstreet's Brigade. After the War, Private Stone moved to Jasper County, Texas, where he was sheriff for over thirty years. (Courtesy Manie Whitmeyer)

FORT SMITH, ARKANSAS, ca. 1900. The man on the right is thought to be Penn Rabb, who lived in Oklahoma. Photographed at Gannaway Studio. (Courtesy Butch Moxley and Lynn Moxley)

BRINKLEY, ARKANSAS, ca. 1901. One finds it difficult to understand how such a lovely portrait can end up in a cardboard box full of photographs marked "one dollar each." This charming little girl is probably about nine or ten years old and, if the careful attention given her hair and clothing is any indication, probably comes from a family who cares a great deal for her. The picture was bought in an antique store.

NASHVILLE, TENNESSEE, ca. 1908. The same girl, now a charming southern belle of sixteen or seventeen. The photographer at Taylor Studio in Nashville managed to coax a faint smile from her exquisite porcelain face.

BIRMINGHAM, ALABAMA, 1925. Fire destroys the old City Hall at Fourth Avenue and 19th Street North. In addition to city offices, the Birmingham Public Library was located in this building.

ALGIERS, LOUISIANA, ca. 1895. From the Brennan Studio, which occupied a space at 809 Canal Street in New Orleans, this picture of ten-year-old Roy Schroder appears to have been taken at the time of his confirmation in the Church.

MINERAL WELLS, TEXAS, ca. 1893. A family portrait from the Jericho Photo Company in Mineral Wells.

WILSON, NORTH CAROLINA, ca. 1906. A gathering of Wilson County's Confederate veterans. Photographed in front of the Farmers Tobacco Warehouse, these old soldiers were living legends, each with his own story of the War. Notice the two young admirers in the foreground who have crept into the picture to be near their heroes. On the second row, under the large "A", the man in the light uniform proudly holds their Confederate battle flag, barely visible in the photograph. (Courtesy Hugh Johnston and the Captain Jesse S. Barnes Camp, Sons of Confederate Veterans)

DALLAS, TEXAS, October 5, 1881. (Next page) In the studio of J.W. Davis, located on Main Street, George W. Loomis was photographed in this striking pose, a nonchalant stance so popular with the photographers of the 1880s.

SUMTER COUNTY, GEORGIA, ca. 1870. Thomas D.A. Phillips, thirty-five years old in this portrait, was a veteran of Company C, 12th Georgia Infantry, Cook's Brigade, Army of Northern Virginia. He enlisted June 13, 1861, in Macon County, Georgia, and after four years of battling the enemy, surrendered with Robert E. Lee at Appomattox. (Courtesy Hunter Phillips)

KENTUCKY, ca. 1910.

ST. LOUIS, MISSOURI, ca. 1895. Many a southern boy attended military school in the South's numerous military academies. This handsome young cadet had his picture made in the studio of F.W. Guerin, located at 409 North Broadway.

ST. LOUIS, MISSOURI, ca. 1890. "Cousin Ella Guerin." Probably a relative of the photographer, F.W. Guerin.

DRAKE, OKLAHOMA, ca. 1920. Three young musicians from the little community of Drake which today is no more than a crossroads settlement. In the rural part of Murray County, it is located two miles north of Nebo, another crossroads community, or about twelve miles north east of the large city of Gene Autry, population 178.

HILLSVILLE, VIRGINIA, ca. 1910. Jack and George Tolbert. (Courtesy Larry Alderman)

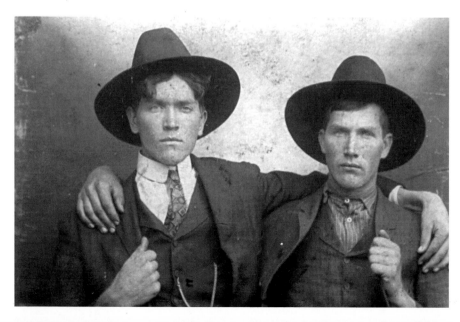

BELLEVIEW, TENNESSEE, ca. 1918.

VICKSBURG, MISSISSIPPI, ca. 1880s. (Next page) The *Tennessee Belle,* a steamboat belonging to the New Orleans-Vicksburg Packet Company, loading up bales of cotton, probably headed for New Orleans. Packet boats carried mail, cargo, and passengers. This picture is thought to have been taken at the dock in Vicksburg.

LEESVILLE, LOUISIANA, 1905. A group of young ladies from East Texas were visiting their cousins in Leesville when they decided that the whole group should have its picture made. (Courtesy Manie Whitmeyer)

HENDERSONVILLE, NORTH CAROLINA, ca. 1900. Little babies, whether boy or girl, were dressed in long, lacy dresses. This little one couldn't keep his left hand still for his sitting at Baker Studio.

CLEBURNE, TEXAS, 1909. Garland Douglass in her brand new Easter dress. This photograph was mounted on a handsomely embossed cabinet card from the studio of J.T. Davis.

MISSOURI, ca. 1912. Four of the Kimberlin brothers: I.J., W.G., P.S., and J.N. The younger brother, J.N., relates an early incident of the War.

My father and four brothers went out early in the defense of the South. I was too young at that time, but remained at home and did all that I was able to do for Quantrill. Father was severely wounded, which disabled him for active service, and he came back home to nurse his wounds. . . . The Federal Commander, Colonel Pennock, by some means learned that father was at home suffering from wounds, and at once began a scheme to capture him. We had a neighbor named Massey, who was a sympathizer with the Federal army. He and father had been for years close friends. Pennock, having gained this information, at once sought out Massey and had him go to my father and pretend great friendship for him and advise that if my father would come in and surrender and take the oath of allegiance he could then return home and remain under the protection of the United States flag.

After considering the proposition made by Pennock through the lying, deceptive Massey, my father accepted the offer, and in company with Massey went direct to the Colonel's quarters. Immediately on my father's being introduced, Pennock turned to one of his guards and said: "Put this old devil in jail." On the following morning father was sent under guard out home, where he was brutally hanged in his own barn amid the cries and pleadings of my heartbroken mother and her helpless children.

This was September 2, 1862. The home was then stripped of its contents and burned to the ground. The barn, having a great deal of feedstuff stored therein, was not burned at that time; but about two weeks later, after hauling all the feed away, the barn was burned. Not content with what they had already done, they set fire to the rail fence around the farm and burned it to the ground.

About one month after the brutal murder of my father these same robbers captured old man Sanders and another old gentleman named Crawford and brought them to where my mother then lived and killed them both in our yard. Mr. Sanders was about seventy-three years old and Mr. Crawford was about three years younger.

(*Confederate Veteran*, November, 1912)

SULPHUR SPRINGS, TEXAS, December 19, 1897. A wedding photograph of John Washington Eitel and Jessie Lee Bone.

DENISON, TEXAS, April 9, 1894. All dressed up in his knickers — the style of the day — this fourteen-year-old southern boy posed at the Macurdy Studio, 103 West Main, in Denison. On the back of the photo, written most likely in his own hand, is this pencilled message: *Finley Booker, to Eddie Hamer, Caddo, I.T.* Caddo was a small town across the Red River over in Indian Territory, about thirty miles northeast of Denison.

COLLEGE PARK, GEORGIA, ca. 1888. The Victorian residence of H.M. Abbett, located at 207 East
Virginia Avenue.

RICHMOND, VIRGINIA, ca. 1910. Reunion photo of the Robert E. Lee Camp Number One, United
Confederate Veterans. These wonderful old heroes are all neatly dressed in their UCV uniforms.

ARKANSAS, ca. 1870s. This was a popular pose of the times — man seated with woman standing to his left, her hands resting upon his shoulder.

NASHVILLE, TENNESSEE, 1900. Cora Alsup, with her diploma. Students used to graduate from the eighth grade, then go on to high school or go to work. Eighth-grade graduation ceremonies were very important and almost universal in the South. (Courtesy Edwin P'Pool)

DUBLIN, GEORGIA, ca. 1895. This handsome southern gentleman has what southerners called a "chiseled face," as if his classic features had been cut from the finest stone by an expert sculptor. Southerners described northerners as "ferret-faced and beady-eyed." This photo was made by photographer John D. Smith.

WETUMKA, OKLAHOMA, ca. 1930. Vida Burkes, a beautiful lady — and a fashionable one.

MONTGOMERY, ALABAMA, 1919. Members of The First White House Association look on while Gov. Thomas E. Kilby signs an appropriation bill from the Alabama legislature, making $25,000 available for moving and restoring the first White House of the Confederacy. The house was moved near the state capitol in 1920, and the dedication service was held on June 3, 1921. The people of Alabama, whose state had been ravaged by Reconstruction, have to be admired, not only for pulling themselves up by their own bootstraps to a point where they could once again produce an economy that was able to feed its people, but also for making the sacrifices necessary for preserving their rich Confederate heritage.

MONTGOMERY, ALABAMA, ca. 1929. The parlors inside the First White House of the Confederacy. Forty-seven years later, funds were obtained to give the White House a major restoration. Work began in April, 1976. Mistakes made in 1921 were corrected, and steel beams were put under both floors to support the 100,000 visitors who view the house each year. New heating, plumbing, cooling, and electrical systems were installed. Above all, architectural details and interior decor were authenticated. On December 10, all was ready, and Alabama presented its bicentennial gift to posterity. A descendant of President Tyler raised the Stars and Bars while the Maxwell Air Force Band played. Throngs of people heard the speakers — Gov. George Wallace and Bertram Hayes-Davis, great-great-grandson of Jefferson Davis. A cannon volley saluted the ribbon-cutting, and the fife and drum corps played "Dixie." Today, the White House is elegantly furnished with actual furnishings used by the Davises. It stands as a proud symbol of the dignified culture of the short-lived Confederate States of America.

LITTLE ROCK, ARKAN-SAS, February, 1898. Information on the back reads: *Miss Black, 1201 Broadway Street.*

FLORIDA, 1905. Taken from a stereoscope card, this is the view one might have found along the inland creeks of old Florida. Alligators freely roamed the mirrored waterways of this subtropical paradise. Pollution was unknown. The ecological balance was perfect until man began draining the swamps, pouring concrete, and dumping refuse. Paradise lost.

BONHAM, TEXAS, December 14, 1909. Clay Whited and Winnie Johnson on their wedding day. Clay and Winnie were first cousins, their mothers being sisters. Even though most people considered such situations unusual, there was precedent for it among the Scottish clans from which many southerners were descended. McRae was the maiden name of Clay's mother, Caroline Whited, and Winnie's mother, Della Johnson. Although primarily of Scottish descent, Clay and Winnie were both one-sixteenth Cherokee. From a line of long-lived people, Clay lived to be 88 years old, while Winnie lived to a ripe old age of 99. Today, they rest side by side in their ancestral burial grounds — the old Round Prairie Cemetery at Elwood, Texas.

WETUMKA, OKLAHOMA, ca. 1915. (Next page) The Kozy, a drug store located on the west side of Main Street. Even though most people called these places drugstores, they were also more correctly called confectionaries or soda shoppes when, like this one, they did not sell prescription drugs. Andrew Burkes, the owner, stands in front of the counter. His brother, Hilliard, draws a soft drink from the fountain behind the counter. Cigars are in the case to the right, chocolate and coconut candy in the showcase to the left. It appears to be September, for tablets, bottles of ink, and other school supplies have been laid out on the tables in the foreground.

TENNESSEE, ca. 1898. Edward Ward Carmack, who represented Tennessee in the U.S. House of Representatives from 1898 until 1901, was elected by the Tennessee General Assembly to become U.S. Senator, a post he held from 1901 until 1907. One of Tennessee's best-known, best-loved public representatives, he is most widely remembered today for his eloquent address before the House of Representatives on April 22, 1898, where he ended his remarks with what has become known as Carmack's Pledge to the South. In a tragic twist of fate, he was denied the peaceful end of which he had so fondly spoken. On November 9, 1908, as he left his office and started towards home, two of his political enemies approached him. Having spotted a lady acquaintance, Carmack was raising his hat and bowing to her when the murderers fired two bullets into his body, killing him instantly. Rarely has Tennessee mourned the loss of a public figure as it did in the passing of Edward Ward Carmack. Gracing the statehouse grounds is an impressive statue of the great Carmack, and upon its pedestal is written his immortal tribute to Dixie.

# Carmack's Pledge to the South

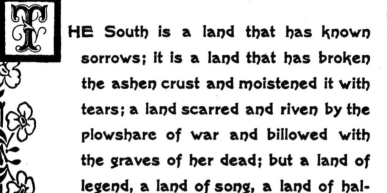

**T**HE South is a land that has known sorrows; it is a land that has broken the ashen crust and moistened it with tears; a land scarred and riven by the plowshare of war and billowed with the graves of her dead; but a land of legend, a land of song, a land of hallowed and heroic memories.

**T**O that land every drop of my blood, every fiber of my being, every pulsation of my heart, is consecrated forever.

**I** was born of her womb; I was nurtured at her breast; and when my last hour shall come, I pray God that I may be pillowed upon her bosom and rocked to sleep within her tender and encircling arms.

SAN ANTONIO, TEXAS, 1917. Ward Henry, a well-to-do bachelor, standing beside his Chevrolet touring car.

PULASKI, TENNESSEE, ca. 1910. Captain John Booker Kennedy was one of the six young men who organized the original Ku Klux Klan on Dec. 24, 1865, in the law office of Judge Thomas M. Jones. Little then did they realize that their newly formed social club would become the awesome force which eventually overthrew carpetbag rule in the South. Kennedy is also credited with naming the group. (See pages 323-325.)

BEAUMONT, TEXAS, ca. 1900. Made by Holland's Studio. Message on the back reads: *Margaret and Mr. Landis in a decorated trap in the floral parade in Beaumont.*

TENNESSEE, ca. 1915. William Ferrol Black, a Confederate veteran shown here wearing his Southern Cross of Honor, awarded by the UDC. In 1862, at the age of sixteen, he had joined Co. B, 7th Tennessee Cavalry, coming under the command of Gen. Nathan Bedford Forrest, with whom he served until the end of the War. (*Confederate Veteran*, September, 1920)

CARROLL COUNTY, VIRGINIA, ca. 1910. Cora Farmer's daughter. (Courtesy Larry Alderman)

ALEXANDER, ARKANSAS, ca. 1895. Photograph was made by photographer Henry Holland.

THONOTOSASSA, FLORIDA, ca. 1930. Paul Ivie.
(Courtesy Darlene Trent)

DUPLEX, TENNESSEE, ca. 1910. (Opposite page) In the South, churches used to have what was called an "All-Day Singin' and Dinner-on-the-Ground," or, in some cases, "All-Day Preachin' and Dinner-on-the-Ground." In the rural South, one can occasionally find one of these events today. Folks arrive for Sunday morning worship, bearing home-cooked food, and remain for most of the day. At noon, everyone gathers under the trees, where the delicious food has been set out on long tables, hardly able to wait for someone to holler out, "Brother _____, (usually the preacher or a deacon) would you offer thanks so we can get started on this food?" At the end of what you are hoping is a real short prayer, one of the women who seems to be sort of unofficially in charge calls out, "Let the men go first!" No instructions are needed from that point on. You fill up your plate and look for a comfortable spot on the ground. The eatin' meetin' depicted in these two wonderful old photos took place at the Mt. Carmel Cumberland Presbyterian Church at the little cross-roads community of Duplex. The church is still in use today and looks much as it did in 1910. The man standing to the left of the table, looking back at the camera, is Clint Thompson. (Courtesy James M. Thompson)

VIRGINIA, ca. 1862. General Joseph Reid Anderson, shown here in his Confederate uniform, was a West Point graduate, class of 1836. When the War broke out, he was commissioned brigadier general and put in command at Wilmington, North Carolina. In the spring of 1862, he returned to Virginia, where he resigned his commission on July 19 and returned to the Tredegar Iron Works. It was through his expertise there that he was able to render invaluable service to the Confederacy. His company became the mainstay of the Confederate Ordnance Department until the closing days of the War, ceasing operations only upon the evacuation of Richmond.

LEXINGTON, KENTUCKY, ca. 1900. The stone courthouse of Fayette County. In 1911, the equestrian statue of Confederate hero John Hunt Morgan would be added to the front lawn on the far side of the front steps.

WYNNEWOOD, OKLAHOMA, ca. 1917. A snapshot of E.L. Courtney in his Reo automobile. (Courtesy LaRuth Mackey and Ann Robberson)

DECATUR, TEXAS, ca. 1900. This is the Ramsey family, George and Sarah and their children — Bess (the little girl), Buren, and Roe. Photograph made at the Haddix Studio in Decatur.

MANSFIELD, TEXAS, ca. 1900. This little charmer exhibits the typical summer dress of a southern boy — overalls, cotton shirt, and a straw hat. Boys went barefooted in the summertime, and those who could afford it got a new pair of shoes when school started in the fall. This same type of attire was common well into the 1950s in small towns and rural areas all across Dixie.

NASHVILLE, TENNESSEE, ca. 1889. Photograph made in the studio of W.G. and A.J. Thuss, located at 228 and 230 North Cherry.

CARROLL COUNTY, VIRGINIA, ca. 1900. It was probably this type of horse-drawn hearse that the composer had in mind when he wrote *Will the Circle Be Unbroken*? One of the verses is especially poignant.

> Undertaker, undertaker,
> Undertaker, please drive slow,
> For that body you are haulin' —
> Lord, I hate to see her go.

(Courtesy Larry Alderman)

BIRMINGHAM, ALABAMA, 1916. (Next page) A group of Confederate veterans lining a Birmingham street. In the foreground are their ever-present UDC sponsors and three young boys with bugles. All are probably in preparation for a parade, one of the most exhilarating events connected with UCV reunions. (Courtesy Hunter Phillips)

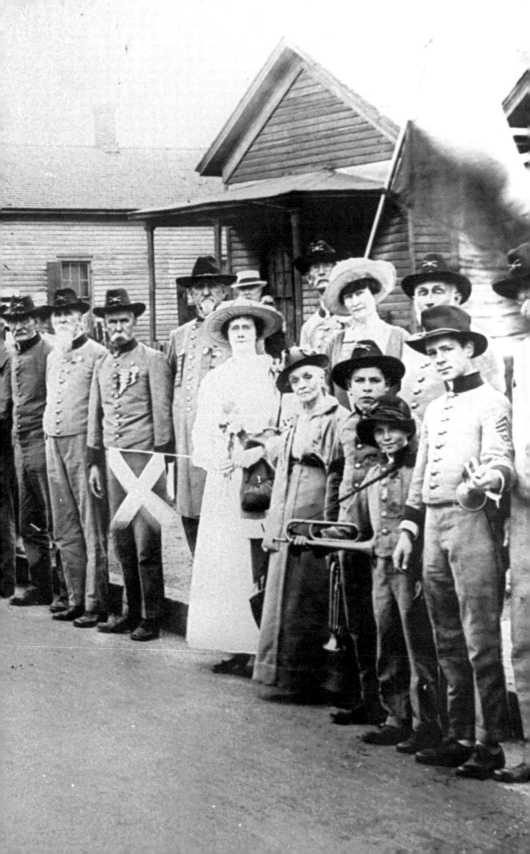

SAN ANGELO, TEXAS, April 30, 1910. This photo is from a postcard addressed to Miss Annie __?__, of Hopkinsville, Kentucky. It reads: *Am having a dandy time out here. Go horseback riding every morning. Are you still with Miss Jennie? See by papers that Mrs. Ragsdale is out. How is Aunt Lizzie? Love to her. Be good.* — Eula.

AUSTIN, TEXAS, June 1, 1898. The twenty-ninth annual reunion of Terry's Texas Rangers (8th Texas Cavalry, CSA) was held at the Driskill Hotel. Among items of business discussed at the meeting was the proposed Confederate monument for the state capitol. After adjourning, the veterans met the governor and the grounds superintendent at the capitol where they were shown the site for the new monument — a choice position in front of the capitol and just opposite the Alamo monument. (*Confederate Veteran*, August, 1898)

SOUTH CAROLINA, ca. 1930. Spanish moss, gray and mysterious, festoons giant oak trees, lending an air of romance to the coastal regions of the Deep South. An epiphytic plant, the moss grows best where humidity is high. It can be found growing naturally as far inland as 225 miles, the area around Shreveport, Louisiana, being a good example. Although it will grow on various types of trees, or even on a fence post, its favorite host is the live oak tree. In contrast to a parasite, Spanish moss is not detrimental to its host for it derives its nutrients from the atmosphere alone.

ARKANSAS, ca. 1906.

NASHVILLE, TENNESSEE, ca. 1920. *Longview*, which had its beginnings in the 1840s as a four-room brick cottage, is Nashville's best example of those splendid old neo-classical homes which have come to typify the Old South and its legendary splendor. Ironically, the facade which gives it that southern, ante-bellum look was not added until 1906, and, oddly enough, most Nashvillians have never seen the house from this view, for it does not front on any street. A small driveway, obscured by trees, leads to the left end of the house from a side street. When built, *Longview* had frontage on the Franklin Pike, but the house and several acres of its front lawn were sold to the Church of Christ in 1949. Eventually, the church built a new building along the pike, blocking the view. Several years ago, the house was sold to an individual who has restored the magnificent place, whittled down from its original 1500 acres to only a couple of acres immediately surrounding the mansion. Large trees encircle the front lawn of the hilltop home, further obscuring the view.

On December 3, 1864, General John Bell Hood began deploying troops south of Nashville in an attempt to liberate the city from the Yankees. For approximately two weeks, Confederate troops were encamped around the house. When they were forced to retreat on December 16, it was said that not a tree was left standing on the *Longview* estate. Two weeks of bitter cold, rain, and sleet had necessitated the cutting of all available firewood for the poorly equipped southern soldiers.

CHATTANOOGA, TENNESSEE, 1887. Charles M. Willingham at the age of 16. Photo made in the Schmedling Studio, at 828 Market Street.

NASHVILLE, TENNESSEE, 1894. Mrs. Caroline Meriwether Goodlett, founder and first president (1894-1895) of the United Daughters of the Confederacy. In reality, Mrs. Goodlett was co-founder of the UDC, for it was a joint project with Mrs. Anna Davenport Raines of Savannah, Georgia, notwithstanding a controversial committee decision of the UDC in 1901 that decided in favor of Mrs. Goodlett as sole founder.

Following Mrs. Goodlett as President-General of the UDC, were:

1—From Tennessee (1895-1896), Mrs. John C. Brown, widow of General Brown.

2—From Virginia (1896-1897), Mrs. Fitzhugh Lee, widow of General Lee.

3—From Texas (1897-1899), Mrs. Katie Cabell Currie, daughter of General W.L. Cabell.

4—From Florida (1899-1901), Mrs. Edwin G. Weed.

WYNNEWOOD, INDIAN TERRITORY, ca. 1905. Variously identified as the
E.L. Spencer Telephone Office and the Wynnewood Telephone Exchange,
located on the second floor of the D.M. Lawrence building, first brick structure in town. The man and woman seated are thought to be Mr. & Mrs. Sam
Ferguson, and the gentleman standing beside the switchboard has been
tentatively identified as either Sid McKinney or Dr. Nisler, a veterinarian
who was killed when he fell out of a window on the second floor of this
same building. (Courtesy Butch Moxley and Lynn Moxley)

DUMFRIES, VIRGINIA, 1862. The sign on the door reads: WIGFALL MESS. This is General Louis T. Wigfall's mess hall when he was in charge of the famed Texas Brigade, while it was in camp near Dumfries during the winter of 1861-1862. The Confederate soldier on the right is James Harvey Herbert, who would be wounded and captured at the Second Battle of Manassas the following August. For the rest of the War he was held prisoner by the Yankees, who often tortured their captives by withholding food, water, clothing, blankets, firewood, medicine, and latrine privileges. Denied protection against disease and the harsh northern winters, approximately 31,000 southern men and boys died unnecessary deaths at the hands of their captors. When held on the battlefront, they were sometimes placed in holding pens in front of Yankee fortifications, to be used as human shields against Confederate cannon. All of this bestiality done with the full knowledge and approval of Abraham Lincoln, who personally instituted a policy of no prisoner exchanges so as to eliminate our soldiers from the field! A modern historian has called Lincoln "America's Stalin." (Courtesy Edwin P'Pool)

Miss Kate Freeman Clark, of Holly Springs, Mississippi, was noticed by a New York artist named William Merrit Chase while he was visiting that north Mississippi town. Convinced by Chase that she should go to New York where she would have the opportunity to improve her skills under his tutelage and be able to sell many of her paintings, she left Holly Springs at the age of 16. After thirty years in New York, not a single painting had sold, and Miss Clark returned to Holly Springs at the age of 46 — never to paint again. It was 1923. She had brought all of her paintings home where they remained until her death in 1958. After her demise, Holly Springs followed the instructions in her will and, using the money she left specifically for that purpose, established an art gallery for the display of her works. This photo of Kate Freeman Clark was made around 1897 in her New York studio.

OWENSBORO, KENTUCKY, ca. 1900. (Opposite page) From left to right, on back row: Ray Jesse, Roy Gabbert, James McKinney, Sterman Lancaster, Preston Haden, Charlie Duncan. The gentleman seated, holding the little boy, is Frank Zinsz. Perhaps this is a group of fraternity brothers. Roy Gabbert is wearing some kind of insignia on his pocket, and Preston Haden seems to be wearing some kind of lapel pin.

OWENSBORO, KENTUCKY, ca. 1900. (Opposite page) Preston Haden, Tobe Phipps, and Will Coleman. This pose was taken at Smeather's Studio, located at 109 West Third Street.

FORRESTS BRIGADE
U·C·V· PARADE · BIRMINGHAM · ALA·

BIRMINGHAM, ALABAMA, 1894. The United Confederate Veterans held their annual reunion in Birmingham, and this is part of the all-important parade of the surviving soldiers. UCV parades were an awesome sight and always well-attended. Riding in the front column is George Washington Sneed Herbert, veteran of both Terry's Texas Rangers and Tennessee's famed Coleman's Scouts. Carrying the Confederate flag and riding next to him (side-saddle, of course) is his daughter, Ella Mai, one of the UDC sponsors of the reunion. (Courtesy Edwin P'Pool)

WINCHESTER, TENNESSEE, ca. 1880. Will Hines. Made in the studio of R.B. Williams.

This picture of Will Rogers was made by White Studio in New York, but Will called Oologah, Oklahoma home. The famous entertainer and humorist was born near Oologah in 1879 to parents of Cherokee descent. His father, who was one-eighth Cherokee, had been a Confederate cavalry officer with Gen. Stand Watie's First Cherokee Mounted Rifles. In this 1916 photograph, Will stands with his trademark, the lariat rope. In addition to starring in movies, wild west shows, and the Ziegfield Follies, Will appeared in his own newspaper column where he poked fun at politicians. When asked by a reporter if he belonged to any organized political party, Will answered, "No, I'm a Democrat."

NASHVILLE, TENNESSEE, ca. 1907. These two little girls were probably in some kind of children's pageant or dance recital. Their photos were taken by Thuss Studio on North Cherry Street.

NASHVILLE, TENNESSEE, May 10, 1900. (Next page) This priceless old photograph was discovered hanging on the wall of a rural home at Thompson's Station, on the Columbia Pike, in 1989. It was unframed and exposed to harsh light, but the images were still in remarkably good condition, and dates and names were still intact. Underneath the large photo, which is mounted on a 16 X 20 inch studio card, are these poignant words; SURVIVORS OF COMPANY B, ROCK CITY GUARDS, MANEY'S FIRST TENNESSEE REGIMENT, CONFEDERATE STATES ARMY.

Company B was one of ten companies mustered into service on May 2, 1861, by Col. Bushrod Johnson, and designated as the First Tennessee Infantry Regiment. Actually, the Rock City Guards, who became Company B, had been in existence as a state militia unit since March 8, 1860. On the evening of April 16, they led a secession parade in Nashville, attracting so many recruits that within two weeks they had tripled their number to about 330.

When organized, the First Tennessee was ordered to Virginia where they participated in the Cheat Mountain campaign in September, 1861. After service with the legendary Stonewall Jackson, they were ordered west on February 17, 1862, arriving at Corinth, Mississippi, in time to participate in the Battle of Shiloh. In addition to smaller engagements throughout the War, the Rock City Guards, as part of the First Tennessee Regiment, saw heavy combat at Perryville, Murfreesboro, Chickamauga, Missionary Ridge, and Kennesaw Mountain. After a brief excursion into Alabama, the First Tennessee was engaged in every action of the army on that dreadful retreat from Dalton into Atlanta. In late 1864, they were participants in the ill-fated Battles of Franklin and Nashville, where the courageous Army of Tennessee was virtually annihilated in its last desperate attempt to liberate the state from the iron grip of the brutal Yankees.

The remnants of the Army of Tennessee fell back to West Point, Mississippi, then made a long and arduous journey across Alabama, Georgia, and South Carolina, finally reaching the lonely command of General Johnston at Bentonville, North Carolina. Following the Battle of Bentonville, Johnston surrendered on April 26, 1865. On May 1, four years after being mustered into service, the Rock City Guards were paroled at Greensboro, North Carolina. Of 1200 men at the beginning of the War, the First Tennessee Regiment counted only 125 survivors at the surrender.

In this 1900 photograph, twenty men of Company B have survived war and the creeping inevitability of old age, to gather in one of those bittersweet reunions where old soldiers cherish the memories of their heroic struggle and lament the loss of their comrades and "the cause."

The lady in the photograph is identified as Vera Shearon, the sponsor. It is most likely that the UDC ladies sponsored this reunion, and it is probably they who have supplied the men with boutonnieres, some made of roses and some of mock orange. These are the faces of the leaders of the South — men who came home to be lawyers, doctors, businessmen, public servants, inventors. Southerners are ever haunted by the awful realization of the countless brilliant minds lost to the South during those four agonizing years when its young men, the flower of southern manhood, were cut down by the angry bullet of the invader.

In the reunion photograph, the two men sitting on the front row are C.A. Thompson and W.S. Sawrie. On the second row are John O. Treanor, Robert C. Handley, S.B. Kirkpatrick, J.M. Turner, and Frank Porterfield. On the third row are Alexander Allison, Theodore Cooley, T.H. Maney, P.B. Steele, M.B. Pilcher, and F.P. Elliott. On the top row are J.E. Nichol, S.B. Shearon, J.H. Wilkes, M.B. Toney, P.H. Manlove, Thomas Gibson, and D.J. Dismukes.

FORT SMITH, ARKANSAS, ca. 1890. Samuel R. Kearn, a minister.

TEXAS, ca. 1908. Drilling a water well. This photo was probably made near Mineral Wells or Weatherford and was made up into a postcard, after the fashion of the day.

NASHVILLE, TENNESSEE, May 25, 1884. (Opposite page) This faded old photograph of the Harding Light Artillery was made by Herstein & Mahon Photographers on the occasion of a dance and dinner at Belle Meade mansion. This unit was organized on January 12, 1861, by Gen. William Giles Harding (builder of Belle Meade), who equipped and armed it for service in the Confederacy. It was reorganized on January 12, 1884, as a militia unit. General Harding and his family can be seen standing beneath the fifth column on the porch.

TALLASSEE, ALABAMA, ca. 1897. From this family group only the two oldest daughters are identified — Lucy, on the left, and Pearl, standing next to her. The family resemblance is striking. All of the children standing have their father's eyes. The little girl holding her dolly has her mother's eyes. Photo made in Bilbrey Studio.

ALABAMA, 1950. (Opposite page) There weren't many veterans of either side still living when this picture was taken. The last veteran to die was a Confederate soldier, Walter Williams, who died in Texas at the age of 117. The identification on this photo reads: *Uncle Riggs Crump, 103. James A. Embry, 92.* Pleasant Riggs Crump, on the left, served with Company A, 10th Alabama Infantry, living to be the last Confederate veteran of Alabama, the last survivor of the Army of Northern Virginia, and the last of the men surrendered at Appomattox. (Courtesy Hunter Phillips)

FORT WASHITA, INDIAN TERRITORY, ca. 1875. Dr. W.S. Burks, a surgeon with the 11th Texas Cavalry, CSA, from 1861 through 1865. Born Aug. 26, 1826, in Kentucky, he went to Texas in 1848, to Fort Washita in 1854, and on to Pauls Valley, I.T., in 1893, where he became a banker.

N. F. DUFF, Hillsboro & Itaska, Tex.

TEXAS, ca. 1895. This unusual picture was bought at an antique mall for the exorbitant price of 50¢ in 1990, nearly 100 years after these two gentlemen posed for it. The photograph was made in the studio of N.F. Duff, who had studios in two north central Texas towns — Hillsboro and Itaska. On the back of the studio card, written in pencil, are these remarks: *dwarf — 21 years, 6 months; giant — 5 years, 3 months.*

TENNESSEE, ca. 1910. Few movie stars have been better looking than this west Tennessee gentleman, immaculately groomed and fashionably dressed.

HOT SPRINGS, ARKANSAS, ca. 1900. (Opposite page)

BEN WHEELER, TEXAS, 1903. (Opposite page) One of those wonderful old family group shots. Here, forty-nine members of the J.W. Beggs family gather at the home of one of the kinfolks to preserve forever the image of one southern family. (Courtesy Bobby Mitchell)

LARGEST LOCOMOTIVE
IN THE WORLD LENG 120 FT 7
WYNNEWOOD OKLA

WYNNEWOOD, OKLAHOMA, ca. 1910. The largest locomotive in the world, measuring 120 feet, 7 3/4 inches in length, making a stop in this small Oklahoma town. The only identifiable man, Harvey Allen Halford, is standing just this side of the cowcatcher. (Courtesy Ruth Halford Gammill)

GADSDEN, ALABAMA, ca. 1912. (Opposite page) Confederate veterans of Etowah County are gathered on the courthouse steps for this reunion photograph. William Foster Kennedy is the second man from the right on the third row. In June, 1861, he enlisted in Company D, 10th Alabama Infantry, and was wounded five times during the War — one wound caused by a bullet through the thigh while he was making the ill-fated Pickett's Charge at Gettysburg. Kennedy's son, Fred, who is 87 years old, is a reenactor with the 3rd Alabama Dismounted Cavalry. (Courtesy Hunter Phillips)

LEXINGTON, VIRGINIA, ca. 1938. (Opposite page) Reflective of the southern colonial architecture predominant at Washington and Lee University is this professor's home. The institution began as Augusta Academy in 1749. During the patriotic fervor of 1776, it was renamed Liberty Hall. In 1796, George Washington endowed the school with a gift of stock valued at $50,000; whereupon, the college was renamed Washington Academy — and eventually Washington College — in his honor. After the War Between the States, Robert E. Lee accepted the position of president, serving in that capacity until his death in October, 1870. Shortly afterwards, the school was again renamed to do honor to the memory of its most able and dedicated administrator.

TYLER, TEXAS, 1890. An unidentified man and his moustache. No wonder they had to drink out of moustache cups! The studio of H.R. Farr produced this image.

TYLER, TEXAS, ca. 1895. Same man, same town, same moustache! This time, in a pensive pose, he was photographed at the Harper Studio.

ST. LOUIS, MISSOURI, ca. 1898. These two little girls were photographed at the Murillo Studio, 1314 Olive Street. They're probably sisters who may have been readied for this wonderful pose by the loving hands of their mother. Notice the dresses of lace, hair carefully done up in ringlets, and the pretty little bows framing these two sweet faces — the kind of image that would inspire the popular song of a later period, *Thank Heaven for Little Girls*.

BONHAM, TEXAS, 1900. Two beautiful little girls, Queenie Verlie and Cecil Hope Burkes, daughters of Andrew and Eulalie Burkes. Queenie Verlie died shortly after this picture was taken and was buried in the cemetery at Telephone, Texas. Photo was taken at the C.E. Foster Studio.


SELMA, ALABAMA, 1915. (Next page) Confederate veterans and their UDC sponsors at a UCV Reunion. In the center of the stage there appears to be a framed portion of an authentic First National Flag of the Confederacy. (Courtesy Hunter Phillips)

OKLAHOMA, ca. 1916. (Opposite page) "From A.F. and T.A. McRae and family, to Della Johnson and family. We wish you a merry Xmas and a happy New Year. Aunt Della, give the rest of these pictures to the ones their names are on — Eula." A popular custom of the day, sending a family group photo to the kinfolks, brought this family together somewhere in Oklahoma — most likely in Wetumka or Altus. In 1902, they had moved out of north Texas into the Indian Territory, and several copies of this picture were going back to the aunts and uncles left behind. Alexander Franklin McRae and his wife, Texas Adeline Wyatt, had nine girls — no boys. At the time of this picture the girls were probably all married. From left to right are: Estella Thompson, Eulalie Burkes, Edna Burkes, Pearl Spencer, Clara Brady, and Nellie Powell. On the front row are: Ruby Wilcox, Mr. McRae, Opal Dennis, Mrs. McRae, and Jessie Hall. Eulalie and Edna had married brothers. The date of this photograph was determined by Eula's black dress. Her husband, Andrew, had passed away on July 18, 1916, and she was still in mourning when the family sat for this portrait.

MISSISSIPPI, ca. 1910. The *Kate Adams,* a side wheeler, delivering the mail on the Mississippi River. This small community may be Friars Point, Mississippi. (Courtesy Mississippi Department of Archives & History)

TENNESSEE, ca. 1880s. (Opposite page) This little girl's photograph was made as she lay dead in her little bed. She is dressed for burial, holding a bouquet in her tiny hands. As was the custom of the time, the wake was held in the house, a family member sitting up with the body around the clock until the time of the funeral. Perhaps the family had neglected to have the little girl's picture made while she was living. Her death image was made on a tintype, and the damage spots seen here were made by rust.

RALEIGH, NORTH CAROLINA, 1922. G.F. Beavers and George L. Cathey, in front of their cottage at the Confederate Home of North Carolina. Captain Cathey is 101 years old in this picture. At the end of the War, he turned his sword over to his lieutenant for, as he stated, "I couldn't surrender to a Yankee." He attributed his long life to "temperance in all things." (*Confederate Veteran*, February, 1923)

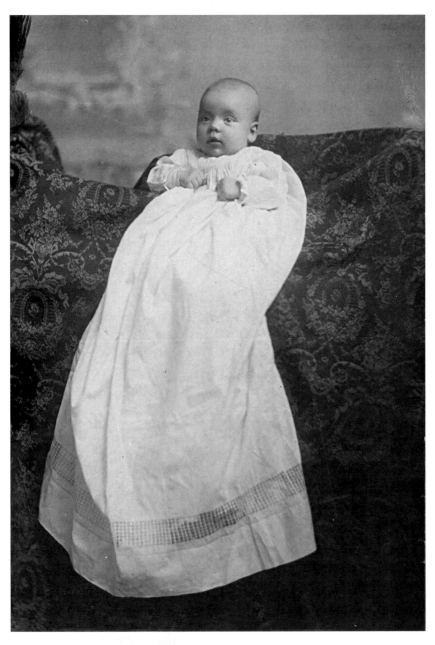

CHATTANOOGA, TENNESSEE, ca. 1890.

KNOXVILLE, TENNESSEE, ca. 1890's. This may be a wedding picture. The man on the left, wearing the white tie, is sporting a new wedding ring. The gentleman sitting is probably his best man. The photo was made in the Weiser Studio, occupying a small space at 119$^1/_2$ Gay Street.

GAINESVILLE, TEXAS, ca. 1906. "Cousins of John Burks, father of Rowena Burks." Made in the Goben Studio.

PAULS VALLEY, OKLAHOMA, ca. 1924. The popularity of the automobile added the roar to the Roaring '20s. Things called garages were springing up behind many a house, and the garage apartment came into vogue — a small apartment located above a two-car garage. Homer L. Hurt, a local attorney and District Attorney of Garvin County, is seated behind the wheel. His wife, Early B. Hurt, sits beside him. Mrs. Hurt taught in the consolidated schools outside of Pauls Valley, as married teachers were not allowed to teach in the city schools. (Courtesy Helen Crawford)

CLEBURNE, TEXAS, ca. 1897. "Mom's flame. Myrtle Taylor's boy-friend when Myrtle lived in Texas." Produced by Bennett Photographers.

TULLAHOMA, TENNESSEE, ca. 1900. John Short, a log hauler. (Courtesy Edwin P'Pool)

NORTH CAROLINA, ca. 1913. A home in the mountains.

LITTLE ROCK, ARKANSAS, ca. 1887.

DUPLEX, TENNESSEE, 1909. The Clinton C. Thompson family. From left to right, Grace, Ruth, Clinton, Roy, Ira (Mrs. Thompson), and baby Clifton. (Courtesy James M. Thompson)

WHITESBORO, TEXAS, August 5, 1915. (Opposite page) A reunion of Confederate soldiers who rode with the 11th Texas Cavalry during the War. Begun in 1878, when the men were only in their thirties, forties, and fifties, these important rendezvous had gone on uninterrupted for 38 years. In this photo, the youngest conceivable age could have been no less than the upper 60s, while most of the aging gentlemen were probably hovering around both sides of the 80-year mark. The only identifiable man is John Calhoun Stribling, fifth from the right on the first row. Ironically, he had served with the 13th Texas Cavalry rather than the 11th. (Courtesy Paul Mott)

WYNNEWOOD, INDIAN TERRITORY, ca. 1901. John Calhoun Stribling, seated, and his son, John Lee Stribling, standing behind him. The girls may be Ella and Leona, probably daughters of the elder Stribling. At the age of 90, John Calhoun Stribling passed away and was buried in Oaklawn Cemetery in Wynnewood, where his grave is marked with a marble Confederate headstone. A large Confederate battle flag flies from the main flag pole in honor of Stribling and more than forty other Confederate soldiers buried in the city cemetery. (Courtesy Paul Mott)

COVINGTON, GEORGIA, ca. 1895. These two wonderful Georgia boys must be brothers, if resemblance counts for anything. Photo is a product of Perkins Studio. (Courtesy Carol Tenpenny)

JONESBORO, TENNESSEE, ca. 1870. Colonel Robert H. Dungan and his wife, formerly Susan Virginia Baker. Enlisted as First Sergeant with the Smyth County Rifle Grays at Seven Mile Ford, Virginia, in 1861, Col. Dungan was colonel of his regiment, the 48th Virginia Infantry,when he surrendered with Robert E. Lee at Appomattox. A few years after the War, he moved to Jonesboro where he founded the Jonesboro Male Institute in order to train the disillusioned young men of the impoverished South. (*Confederate Veteran*, December, 1931)

GADSDEN, ALABAMA, 1914. (Next page) A reunion of Emma Sansom UCV Camp Number 275. Only one veteran, William F. Kennedy, is identified in this assemblage at the Emma Sansom monument. Kennedy, who served with the 10th Alabama Infantry, is seventh from the right on the front row. Emma Sansom climbed upon General Nathan Bedford Forrest's horse and rode behind him out through a field on May 2, 1863, to show him a hidden crossing on the Black Creek. He was desperately trying to get across the river and gain the rear of the Yankees, who had burned the only bridge in the area. Only sixteen years old, brave Emma dismounted with Forrest and crept through the bushes to the edge of the creek to point out the low water crossing. Her efforts aided Forrest in capturing the Indiana colonel and his whole force of 2,000 cavalrymen. For risking life and limb in defense of the cause, Emma was awarded 600 acres of land by the Alabama legislature in 1899, as a token of "admiration and gratitude." But, Emma had married and gone to Texas after the War, and it is doubtful that she ever realized any profit from the gift. She died August 9, 1900, and lies buried at Little Mound, in Upshur County, Texas. During the incident at Black Creek, a soldier had been killed, and Gen. Forrest left the body with Emma for proper burial. Sometime later, Emma wrote about it.

> My sister and I sat up all night watching over the dead soldier, who had lost his life fighting for our rights, in which we were overpowered but never conquered. General Forrest and his men endeared themselves to us forever.

(Courtesy Hunter Phillips)

CHARLOTTE, NORTH CAROLINA, ca. 1910. The Charlotte Police Department.
Seated, from left to right, are Hugh Shields, Cliff Bell, J.T. Farrington, J.D. Johnson,
and B.J. Summerow. Standing are M.M. Earnhart, Charles Ayers, Lee Hargett,
J.E. Crowell, and J.M. Earnhart.

COLUMBUS, MISSISSIPPI, ca. 1912. (Opposite page)

ALABAMA, ca. 1914. Fred Allison Pickrell. (Courtesy Gordon Pickrell)

WETUMKA, INDIAN TERRITORY, ca. 1906. Dr. Abraham Jackson Grissom, Wetumka's first doctor, posed for this picture at the Maynard Studio.

NASHVILLE, TENNESSEE, ca. 1900. (Courtesy Edwin P'Pool)

(Opposite page) Gene Autry, shown here on his famous horse Champion in a publicity photo taken about 1934, was born in Tioga, Texas, on September 29, 1907. With a degree from Tioga High School, he went to work as a railroad telegraph operator in Sapulpa, Oklahoma. Four years later, in 1929, he began his meteoric career by recording the first of his legendary cowboy songs. Gene starred in 82 movies as the singing cowboy, acting out every school boy's dream on the silver screen. In the '30s, '40s, and '50s, he became the perfect role model for the youth of America. In those days, not only did the good guys always win, but the good guys were good. And no one in the industry set a higher moral standard than Gene Autry. He once owned a large ranch in southern Oklahoma near the little town of Berwyn, a community so impressed with the popular cowboy that they changed the name of the town to Gene Autry. A southern boy, he took his southern standards with him, leaving an indelible mark on the history of Hollywood.

Geronimo and his band of Apache guerillas terrorized settlers in the arid southwestern portion of the country. Mexican troops murdered his family in 1858, touching off his ferocious raids. This photo may have been taken in 1895 after he was moved back to Ft. Sill from an Alabama prison. (See pages 196-197.)

———◆———

The Five Civilized Tribes of the Old South (Cherokee, Chickasaw, Choctaw, Creek, and Seminole) were moved into what was considered the western frontier — Indian Territory — during a thirteen-year period beginning in 1827. By 1840, virtually all of the five tribes had been relocated and given title to new lands comprising the present-day state of Oklahoma. Having been engaged in the same business ventures, primarily agricultural, as their white counterparts, they naturally brought with them the implements of their trade, their slaves, and their knowledge of plantation operations. In short, the culture of the Old South was reinstituted in the Indian Territory.

When war broke out in 1861, all of the five tribes enacted their own form of secession by breaking their treaties with the Federal Government and signing anew with the Confederacy. At the end of a losing war, Reconstruction fell like an ax upon the people of the Indian Nation. Reconstruction treaties were harsh, and Federal troops were stationed in the territory to enforce them. Not only were the slaves to be freed, the Indians were ordered to accept the freedmen into their tribes with full privileges — a reprehensible edict fought by the Indians, somewhat successfully, through the turn of the century. In addition to many other concessions, the tribes lost their rights to remain independent nations and were ordered to begin government under a central authority.

One of the harshest measures forced the Indians to give up approximately half of their lands to the Federal government, thus crowding the Five Civilized Tribes into eastern Oklahoma. Their western lands became known as Oklahoma Territory and were used as a dumping ground for the western plains Indians as they were systematically rounded up and forced upon reservations — those who survived the massacres. And so it was that western Oklahoma, Confederate territory for four years, came to be the prison home of many a "wild west" tribe with names like Apache, Comanche, Kiowa, Arapaho, Cheyenne, Caddo, Wichita, and Kickapoo.

ARKANSAS, February 3, 1914. Hattie and Ralph McCoy.

LOUISVILLE, KENTUCKY, 1906. Union Station, a magnificent stone structure so characteristic of public buildings in the upper South and border states.

BROWNSVILLE, TEXAS, ca. 1865. Marcos Morales. (Courtesy William F. King)

GAINESVILLE, GEORGIA, 1912. Miss Etta Hardeman holds the flag she gave to the Georgia Brigade of Cavalry. Maid of honor for the brigade at Rome, she noticed that they had no flag and determined that they would have one before the Macon Reunion. A few months later — thanks to Miss Etta — they carried a proud new flag in the parade at Macon. (*Confederate Veteran,* November, 1912)

MISSISSIPPI, ca. 1895.
(Courtesy Elmore Greaves)

WYNNEWOOD, INDIAN TERRITORY, 1895. Looking at stereoscope cards, these are ladies of the Athenaeum Club. This photograph was probably taken soon after the club was organized in 1895 — or perhaps even the day of the organizational meeting, which was held in the home of Miss Pearl Bradfield, located at the corner of Juanita and Gardner. Established as a study group, combining literary pursuits with civic activities, the club still meets today. Some of its charter members were Mrs. R.J. Wheeler, Mrs. D.C. Wheeler, Mrs. D.C. Cook, Miss Pearl Bradfield, and Miss Sallie Bradfield. The only two ladies identified in the photograph are Miss Sallie, standing at left, and Miss Pearl, standing next to her. (Courtesy Butch Moxley and Lynn Moxley)

CHARLESTON, SOUTH CAROLINA, 1865. Known as Market Hall, this stately piece of architecture was built in 1841. It has survived the Yankees, the Depression, and Hurricane Hugo. Since 1898, it has housed one of the best Confederate museums in the South. The United Daughters of the Confederacy, who operate the museum, are currently trying to raise the funds needed to repair massive hurricane damage to both the building and its priceless artifacts. (Courtesy James David Altman)

NORTH CAROLINA, ca. 1913. A mountain family.

OKLAHOMA CITY, OKLAHOMA TERRITORY, ca. 1900. This couple was photographed in the Oliver Studio, at 129 Main Street.

NASHVILLE, TENNESSEE, ca. 1880. The *Dora Cabler* on the Cumberland River. When this contact print was developed, the glass negative was inadvertently turned backwards resulting in a reversed image. The name of the boat, lettered across the pilot house, reads backwards. (Courtesy Edwin P'Pool)

GAINESVILLE, GEORGIA, ca. 1908. Ethel Ryan, a student at Brenau College in this north Georgia town.

NASHVILLE, TENNESSEE, ca. 1915. (Next page) A Nashville Gas Company work crew on Joe Johnston Street. Three officials of the company are standing in front of the steam engine used for cleaning out the main lines. Manufactured gas had been in use in Nashville since February 13, 1851, when it was used to light the first streetlight down on the square. The president of the company offered a silk dress to the "first lady who would have her house illuminated with gas." By the end of the year, there were 285 customers. In 1946, natural gas was brought in by pipeline from wells on the King Ranch in Texas. (Courtesy Edwin P'Pool)

ALABAMA, ca. 1863. Private William J. Owen, Co. D, 31st Alabama Infantry, CSA. Dressed in anything they could find, our boys went forth into battle. Arrayed against them was a superbly outfitted U.S. Army, usually outnumbering our forces three to one. The only thing new about Private Owen's outfit is his ammunition belt and his Enfield rifle. (Courtesy Hunter Phillips)

122

NASHVILLE, TENNESSEE, ca. 1862. The image of this old wartime engine, the *V.K. Stevenson,* was reprinted from an old glass negative found in the state archives. (Courtesy Edwin P'Pool)

PULASKI, TENNESSEE, ca. 1905. An inviting view — under the magnolias at one of the beautiful old homes in this southern Tennessee town.

LOUISVILLE, KENTUCKY, ca. 1905. City Hall.

CORINTH, MISSISSIPPI, ca. 1880s. (Opposite page) This family group shot was repro-duced from a tintype purchased at an estate sale of the late Wirt Counce, of Corinth. Notice the characteristically irregular shape of the tin.

NORTH CAROLINA, ca. 1913. (Opposite page) A mountain cabin of square-hewn logs.

125

WYNNEWOOD, INDIAN TERRITORY, ca. 1901. Miss Bonnie Carr, at about the age of sixteen. In 1904, she would become a charter member of the local John H. Reagan Chapter, United Daughters of the Confederacy.

VIRGINIA, July, 1861. These are the confident faces of the southern army shortly before it virtually annihilated the great, blustering, pompous Army of the United States in the first large battle at Manassas Junction. Had these young heroes in gray been able to foresee the years of tribulation awaiting the Confederacy, they surely would have marched on into Washington, taking the city and ending the War within the space of a few days.

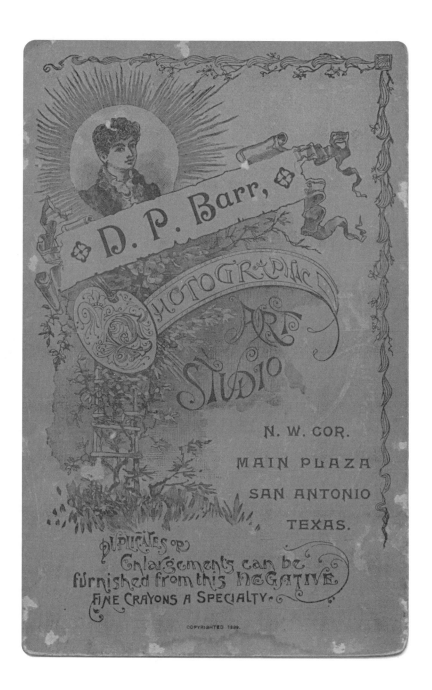

D. P. Barr,

PHOTOGRAPHIC ART STUDIO

N. W. COR.

MAIN PLAZA

SAN ANTONIO

TEXAS.

DUPLICATES OR Enlargements can be furnished from this NEGATIVE. FINE CRAYONS A SPECIALTY.

COPYRIGHTED 1889.

# PART TWO

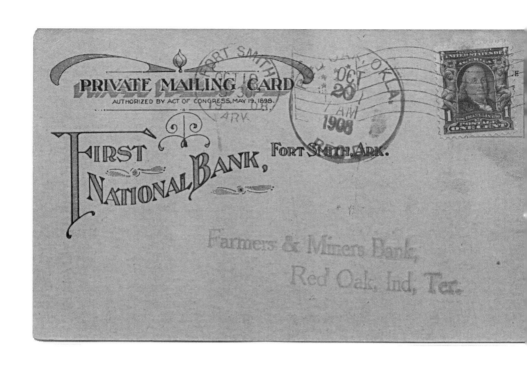

PRIVATE MAILING CARD

AUTHORIZED BY ACT OF CONGRESS, MAY 19, 1898.

FIRST NATIONAL BANK, FORT SMITH, ARK.

Farmers & Miners Bank,
Red Oak, Ind, Ter.

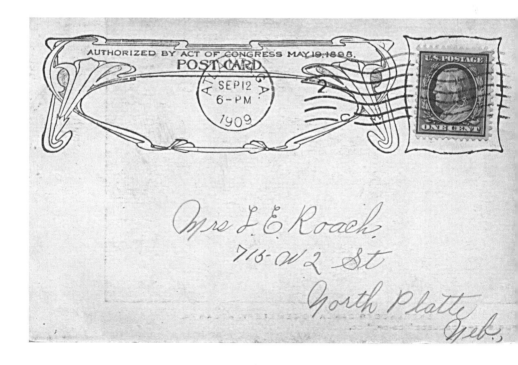

AUTHORIZED BY ACT OF CONGRESS MAY 19, 1898.
POST CARD

Mrs L. E. Roach.
715 W 2 St
North Platte
Neb,

# Post Cards

Postcards are a valuable source of information about the early 20th-century South. They are our eyes into the past of nearly one hundred years ago. While the average southerner was recording the image of his family in a local studio, the postcard was an exciting invitation to the traveling photographer who would unwittingly document the South of that period.

It all began in Vienna on October 1, 1869, when Austria issued the first government postcard in the world. In 1873, the United States allowed its first postcards, which were used primarily by advertisers showing pictures of their products. In 1893, the first official "picture postcards" were issued by Charles Goldsmith, in connection with the Columbian Exposition in Chicago. Pictures of the Exposition appeared on the front, and the address was to be written on the back. No message was allowed.

Then, on May 19, 1898, the U.S. government granted permission to private printers to publish and sell cards, thus ushering in the era of the postcard. These first cards carried restrictions. They were to be posted at one cent each; only name and address were allowed on the reverse side; and, the card had to carry the inscription: *Private Mailing Card Authorized by Act of Congress on May 19, 1898.*

Three and a half years later, on December 24, 1901, the government granted use of the simple term, *Post Card*, on the back of privately printed cards. Any message had to be written on the face of the card. Printers left a small space on the front of the card for a message, but many correspondents got carried away and could not contain their remarks within the limited space, so that many an old postcard of that era shows a picture partially obscured by scribblings of a verbose writer who scrawled indiscriminately.

Finally, on March 1, 1907, the postcard took the form that we know today, when permission was granted for what is called the "divided back." One half of the back side was set aside for a short message, while the other half was reserved for the address and the stamp.

During the early years of this century, the postcard's popularity was unparalleled. Sending, receiving, and collecting them were activities shared by many people, and many a parlor of the late-Victorian period held a common item used for entertaining guests — the postcard album. The golden age of postcards comprised the decade from 1905 to 1915, when collecting cards was at its peak, and it is from that period that we are able to see many views of a beautiful South that, in so many instances, is no more.

In this book, the method of dating each postcard for the reader's information is done primarily by the postmark on the back, giving the exact date the card was mailed. That, of course, does not pinpoint the date of manufacture of the card, for many people wrote on postcards that were five or ten years old; however, in most cases postal cards were used within two to four years of issuance.

In the absence of a postmark — and no correspondence — an attempt is made to determine the actual date of manufacture of the card itself. Keep in mind that the photograph on the postcard might be older yet. Postcards were immensely popular and collectable, giving every community a chance to show off its best architecture and attractions. In the rush to do so, some invariably used photographs at hand, even if they were five or ten years old. Taking that factor into consideration, it must be noted, however, that most communities did try to use current photographs, hence the date of manufacture and the date of the photograph will not be at great variance in many cases.

The postcards reproduced here are shown at actual size.

PLACE
STAMP HERE

Post Card

THIS SIDE FOR THE ADDRESS

BREWTON
NOV 9
8PM
1906
ALA.

Miss Nettie Hood,
c/o J. C. Hood
613 North Street
Jackson
Miss.

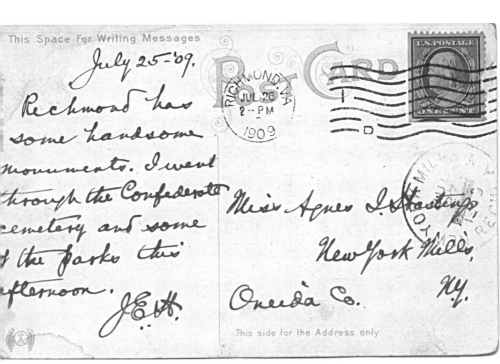

July 25-'09.

Richmond has
some handsome
monuments. I went
through the Confederate
cemetery and some
of the parks this
afternoon. J.E.H.

RICHMOND.VA
JUL 26
2-PM
1909

Post Card

Miss Agnes I. Hastings
New York Mills,
Oneida Co.  N.Y.

This side for the Address only

133

OWENSBORO, KENTUCKY, October 5, 1908. Owensboro College.

HOUSTON, TEXAS, May 4, 1909. Main Street in Houston, showing a residential area. A northern woman, writing to her friend back in Indiana, described Houston. "Everything is so pretty here — flowers everywhere, and all kinds of vegetables. Peaches, fine tomatoes, strawberries, blackberries — only 5 and 10¢ a box. It is offull hot through the day but cool at night."

COLUMBUS, GEORGIA, July 18, 1909. The home of John P. Flournoy, this new house is referred to as a "suburban" home. A most up-to-date residence, it features a water tower of its own.

EUREKA SPRINGS, ARKANSAS, ca. 1907. Most of the buildings in this quaint little Victorian town cling to the side of steep hills. Like many postcards of the era, this one was printed in Germany.

SEBRING, FLORIDA, January 22, 1921. Della, one of those perennial northern sojourn-
ers who flock south during the winter, writes back to one of her frozen friends in
Illinois. "You can see in this picture how strat (Does she mean *straight*?) spanish moss
hangs to the trees. (Does she mean *from* the trees?) Most of the trees are hanging full
of it." She admits that "this moss looks pretty," then in typical Yankee fashion adds,
"but I get tired seeing it everywhere."

Calhoun Monument.
Charleston, S. C.

CHARLESTON, SOUTH CAROLINA, ca. 1915. The monument to John C. Calhoun, South Carolina's preeminent statesman and the South's foremost advocate of states' rights. (See page 368.)

ST. JOSEPH, MISSOURI, September 9, 1909. (Opposite page) This is the house in which Jesse James was living in 1882 when, according to the old song, "that dirty little coward, who shot Mr. Howard, has laid poor Jesse in his grave." After fifteen years of robbing banks and trains, Jesse had been living in retirement as Thomas Howard when a member of his old gang, Robert Ford, shot him in the back of the head. Jesse, who was married and had two children, was only thirty-five years old. No one knows why Jesse and his brother Frank turned to robbery after the War, though some suggest bitterness over Yankees who twice raided their home. Both boys eventually saw service under Confederate guerrilla William Clarke Quantrill.

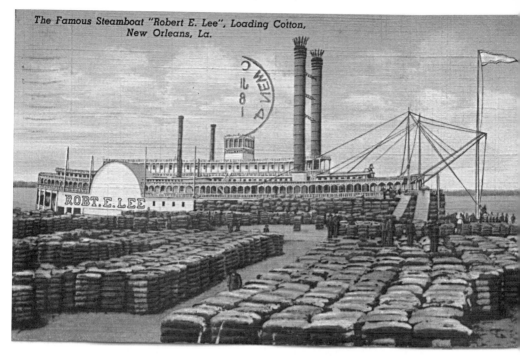

The Famous Steamboat "Robert E. Lee", Loading Cotton,
New Orleans, La.

NEW ORLEANS, LOUISIANA, ca. 1880. Although this postcard is of 1940 vintage, the photograph was taken in the 19th century. Here, the *Robert E. Lee*, made famous by the great steamboat race in 1870, is loading or unloading cotton. On June 30, 1870, the *Robert E. Lee* and the *Natchez* left New Orleans, bound for St. Louis in the greatest steamboat race ever held. Three days, eighteen hours, and fourteen minutes later, the *Robert E. Lee* arrived in St. Louis on the 4th of July, six and a half hours ahead of the *Natchez*.

Cox College, College Park, near Atlanta, Ga.

Calhoun Monument.
Charleston, S. C.

CHARLESTON, SOUTH CAROLINA, ca. 1915. The monument to John C. Calhoun, South Carolina's preeminent statesman and the South's foremost advocate of states' rights. (See page 368.)

ST. JOSEPH, MISSOURI, September 9, 1909. (Opposite page) This is the house in which Jesse James was living in 1882 when, according to the old song, "that dirty little coward, who shot Mr. Howard, has laid poor Jesse in his grave." After fifteen years of robbing banks and trains, Jesse had been living in retirement as Thomas Howard when a member of his old gang, Robert Ford, shot him in the back of the head. Jesse, who was married and had two children, was only thirty-five years old. No one knows why Jesse and his brother Frank turned to robbery after the War, though some suggest bitterness over Yankees who twice raided their home. Both boys eventually saw service under Confederate guerrilla William Clarke Quantrill.

JACKSONVILLE, TEXAS, ca. 1930. Founded as Alexander Institute in 1873 by Dr. Isaac Alexander, this college was endowed in 1924 by Lon Morris, for whom it was renamed.

ASHEVILLE, NORTH CAROLINA, August 28, 1907. The town square, centered on the monument to Zebulon Vance, North Carolina's Confederate governor and distinguished statesman.

CHATTANOOGA, TENNESSEE, ca. 1912. Printed on back of card: *DIXIE SIGHT-SEE-ING AUTOS, CHICKAMAUGA BATTLEFIELDS, CHATTANOOGA, TENN. Take the Dixie Sight-seeing Autos for a three hour trip over Chickamauga Battlefields, Fort Oglethorpe, Ga., and National Cemetery. $1.00 Round Trip.*

RUTHERFORDTON, NORTH CAROLINA, ca. 1930. The First Baptist Church.

*The Famous Steamboat "Robert E. Lee", Loading Cotton, New Orleans, La.*

NEW ORLEANS, LOUISIANA, ca. 1880. Although this postcard is of 1940 vintage, the photograph was taken in the 19th century. Here, the *Robert E. Lee*, made famous by the great steamboat race in 1870, is loading or unloading cotton. On June 30, 1870, the *Robert E. Lee* and the *Natchez* left New Orleans, bound for St. Louis in the greatest steamboat race ever held. Three days, eighteen hours, and fourteen minutes later, the *Robert E. Lee* arrived in St. Louis on the 4th of July, six and a half hours ahead of the *Natchez*.

*Cox College, College Park, near Atlanta, Ga.*

DUNNELLON, FLORIDA, ca. 1930. A little bit of paradise in north central Florida, this is 53-foot Rainbow Falls, about twenty miles from the Gulf Coast.

ATLANTA, GEORGIA, January 13, 1912. (Opposite page) An old postcard showing Cox College in College Park, Georgia. Written from 367 Spring Street in Atlanta, the writer addressed these remarks to A.C. Phillips of Watertown, Tennessee: *Are you dead? or what. Why didn't you come to Atlanta Christmas? I had a grand time. Stayed one short week. We 3 wished for the other. (The Big 4) . . . Write Mr. Nixon, he doesn't know what to think of you. What are you doing?* This magnificent building was built in 1893. Cox College, also known as Southern Female College, occupied the building until the death of Professor Cox, the owner, in 1939. In 1940, the city bought the building and promptly tore it down.

Scene in a Grape Fruit Orchard, Florida.

FLORIDA, ca. 1907. Picking grapefruit in Florida's famous orchards. The postcard at the top of the page was published by H. & W.B. Drew Company of Jacksonville.

Grape Fruit, Florida.

FLORIDA, ca. 1916. Picking oranges. The postcard at the bottom of the page was published by W.J. Harris & Company of St. Augustine.

*Garnett Orange Grove, St. Augustine, Fla.*

36821

"Beaulieu" Herndon Residence, Pass Christian.
(White House of Dixie.)

PASS CHRISTIAN, MISSISSIPPI, January 27, 1917. A lady writes to her friend, Mrs. Joe Perry of Russellville, Kentucky, telling of the flowers blooming and the nice weather on the coast. She points out that this is the place where President Wilson and his family "spent their time while here."

WALNUT RIDGE, ARKANSAS, ca. 1925. The Baptist Church.

Baptist Church, Walnut Ridge, Ark.

1B245

SCENE IN RESIDENCE DISTRICT, SELMA, ALA.

SELMA, ALABAMA, ca. 1916.

TENNESSEE, 1931. This old mill had survived into the 1930s when photographer W.M. Cline took this picture. Sitting right on the edge of a paved road, it was probably located in southern Tennessee, near Chattanooga perhaps.

THE OLD MILL

121041-N

GREENSBORO, NORTH CAROLINA, ca. 1928. A bird's-eye view of the Methodist Episcopal Church South on West Market Street. The Methodist Church split on a north-south basis about fifteen years before the outbreak of the War Between the States. The Methodist Church in the South was thereafter known as the M.E. Church South. It was only in recent times that the two factions were reunited, and many an old cornerstone still reads: M.E. Church South.

"NATIONAL" FIXTURES—M. M. STEPHENSON, DANVILLE, VA.

SNELL ARCADE BUILDING                                    3100-29

ST. PETERSBURG, FLORIDA, January, 1936.

DANVILLE, VIRGINIA, ca. 1916. (Opposite page) Many southerners can remember when the local drug store was as charming as this one. An unusual postcard, this one was put out by the National Show Case Company of Columbus, Georgia, with the following sales pitch printed on the back: *Virginia is noted for its aristocracy, and it is a badge of distinction to be referred to as one of the F.F.V.'s. The Virginia druggists are discriminating in their taste. We are proud of the fact that they look upon National Fixtures as being an aristocrat and worthy of their highest confidence. Mr. M.M. Stephenson was not satisfied until he had installed National Fixtures. We show a view of his beautiful store on the opposite side. Catalogue or salesman upon request.*

147

SHREVEPORT, LOUISIANA, ca. 1916. Holy Trinity Catholic Church.

SHREVEPORT, LOUISIANA, January 13, 1910. St. Mary's Convent is the subject of this postcard sent by H. Brooks to Maud Webster of Lubbock, Texas.

SHREVEPORT, LOUISIANA, ca. 1909. The Baptist Church.

SHREVEPORT, LOUISIANA, ca. 1929. First Methodist Church.

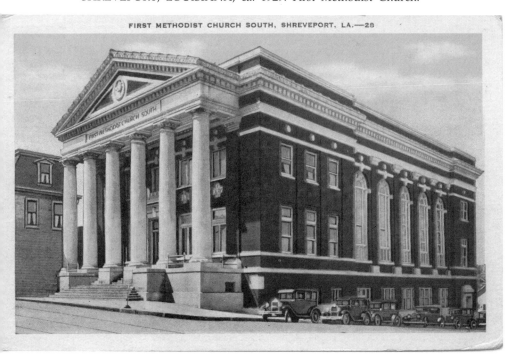

PRICE-WEBB SCHOOL BUILDING. LEWISBURG, TENN.

LEWISBURG, TENNESSEE, ca. 1908. The Price-Webb School.

THOMASVILLE, GEORGIA, ca. 1930. This card shows the First Baptist Church, built in the "southern colonial" style so widely employed in church construction throughout the South during the first quarter of the 20th century.

T-31 FIRST BAPTIST CHURCH, THOMASVILLE, GA.

E-9108

CONFEDERATE ARCH, BLANDFORD CEMETERY, PETERSBURG, VA.

PETERSBURG, VIRGINIA, ca. 1916. The Confederate Arch at Blandford Cemetery in Petersburg, Virginia.

HATTIESBURG, MISSISSIPPI, January 1, 1913. Written by the wife of a man named Hampton back to "The Aunties" at Sharon Grove, in Todd County, Kentucky, this card was published by S.H. Kress & Company.

Confederate Soldiers' Home of Ga., Atlanta, Ga.

ATLANTA, GEORGIA, ca. 1916. The view in this postcard is actually a scale drawing, rather than a photograph, of the Confederate Soldiers' Home in Georgia. Every southern state had such a home for aging veterans who became destitute and would otherwise have had no place to live out their final days. The belligerent government in Washington denied these old men so much as a penny, while our taxes were spent on fatter and fatter pensions for Yankee veterans.

C.T. 14—Typical Charleston Home, Charleston, S. C.
"America's Most Historic City"

CONFEDERATE MONUMENT, SPARTANBURG, S. C.

SPARTANBURG, SOUTH CAROLINA, ca. 1916. The Confederate monument — a country's way of saying thanks to a whole generation of brave men — gladdened the heart of many an old soldier who gazed, through eyes growing dim, at a memorial to his own patriotism.

CHARLESTON, SOUTH CAROLINA, ca. 1935. (Opposite page) The printed inscription on the back of this card describes the unusual custom of building homes that do not face the street. *Here is the Charlestonian type of home, reflecting the early desire for privacy. Note particularly the long veranda facing the southern sea breezes, isolated from the public by a heavy, solid, street door, generally locked, often located at the sidewalk, blocking people from freely entering the porch. Further privacy is provided by high walls, wrought iron grill work and bushes.* Another consideration was that Charlestonians found they could make better use of a small frontage by facing the house to the side yard.

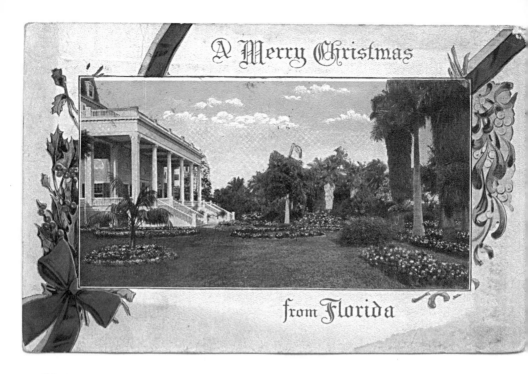

ST. AUGUSTINE, FLORIDA, 1915. A post card, dated Dec. 12, 1915, which was sent by Mrs. J.L. Morgan to a friend in Newton, Illinois. The great winter migrations had obviously already begun, for Mrs. Morgan writes, "I hope to see Newton well represented down here this winter."

JEFFERSON CITY, MISSOURI, ca. 1907. The old state capitol.

SAN ANTONIO, TEXAS, ca. 1920. A view of bustling Houston Street. The movie theater on the left side of the street is showing "Lord Jim."

WILSON, NORTH CAROLINA, ca. 1935. The imposing, modified Greek Revival courthouse of Wilson County was completed in 1924.

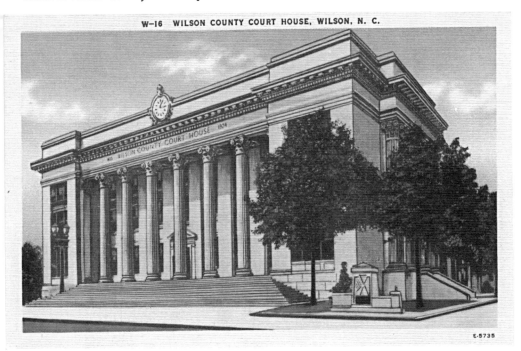

SOMEWHERE IN THE SOUTH, PROBABLY TEXAS, ca. 1910. These men are gathered around the town square awaiting the cotton buyer's inspection of their cotton. It appears to be early fall, so the final picking has probably been completed. Since the cotton here has already been ginned and compressed into 500-pound bales, it is likely that these growers have been holding their bales at home for several weeks waiting for the price of cotton to go up.

Soldiers and Sailors Monument,
(29th and Main Sts.), Richmond, Va.

RICHMOND, VIRGINIA, April 18, 1910. The largest monuments in the South honor the Confederacy. This one is enormous. The column is a counterpart, on a reduced scale, of the famous Pompey pillar at Alexandria, Egypt, and the colossal bronze figure surmounting it is said to be one of the largest pieces of solid bronze ever cast in this country.

FLORIDA, February 27, 1905. (Opposite page) A good view of a neatly kept orange grove, this photograph was made and copyrighted in 1904. From 1898 through March 1, 1907, all messages had to be written on the face of the card, this one being a good example of too little room and too much to say.

BEREA, KENTUCKY, ca. 1940. On the campus of Berea College, this is the Rogers Fine Arts Building, an excellent example of the "southern colonial" style so popular with academic institutions of the South.

BATON ROUGE, LOUISIANA, ca. 1907. St. Joseph's Convent. Minnie Holland sent this card to Amanda Felts in Kevil, Kentucky.

St. Joseph's Convent, Baton Rouge, La.

NATCHEZ, MISSISSIPPI, ca. 1930. The parlor and dining room at *Lansdowne*, built in 1852 by George M. Marshall. This ante-bellum home is still owned by the Marshall family.

JAMESTOWN, VIRGINIA, ca. 1907. In the distance is a vine-covered arbor leading to a colonial and Confederate fort. The granite cross in the foreground was erected in memory of a visit to Jamestown by the General Convention of the Protestant Episcopal Church on October 15, 1898.

ST. PETERSBURG, FLORIDA, ca. 1929. The Baptist Church represents one of the most popular architectural styles used in public buildings during the first quarter of the 20th century — two-story buildings of buff-colored brick, essentially square, flat-topped, with the main floor raised over a street-level basement, and the customary white-columned portico dominating the front of the structure.

SHOWING THE BAR WHERE THE FAMOUS CRAZY WELL WATER IS SERVED, MINERAL WELLS, TEXAS.

Georgia State Monument, Chickamauga Battlefield, Chattanooga, Tenn.

CHATTANOOGA, TENNESSEE, ca. 1912. The Georgia monument at Chickamauga Battlefield. Printed on back of card is the monument's inscription. *To those who fought and lived, to those who fought and died, to those who gave much, to those who gave all — Georgia erects this monument.*


MINERAL WELLS, TEXAS, November 10, 1921. (Opposite page) This is the counter at the Crazy Well Drinking Pavilion. The signs over the back bar describe each mineral water drink. *FOR BRIGHTS DISEASE, Diabetes & all Nervous Trouble, CRAZY NO. 1 CANNOT BE SURPASSED./FOR SOUND SWEET SLEEP, DRINK CRAZY NO. 2./CRAZY NO. 3 FOR PROMPT ACTION ON THE LIVER/When A Strong Cathartic IS REQUIRED, DRINK CRAZY NO. 4.*

First Baptist Church, Paragould, Ark.

5240-29-N

PARAGOULD, ARKANSAS, ca. 1920. First Baptist Church. This magnificent type of church architecture was common throughout the South during the early part of the 20th century, and fine examples can still be seen in communities where church leaders have had the foresight to preserve, rather than destroy, these architectural gems.

GALVESTON, TEXAS, ca. 1916. A magnificent Victorian home. Postcard published by Seawall Specialty Company of Galveston.

A Winter Home, Galveston, Tex.

PERKINS, OKLAHOMA, ca. 1910. In the upper photo, cotton wagons are lined up awaiting their turns at the cotton gin. Below, the gin can be seen in the background. (Courtesy Butch Moxley and Lynn Moxley)

BRADENTON, FLORIDA, ca. 1916. An old street scene typical of the quaint, small towns of the South. With the exception of automobiles, this vignette remained virtually unchanged through the 1950s. The 1960s ushered in the era of urban renewal, shopping malls, and violent social change which, combined, destroyed the homogeneity — and consequently the tranquility — of the southern community.

MAIN BUILDING, ALABAMA POLYTECHNIC INSTITUTE

Florida State Monument,
Chickamauga Battlefield, near Chattanooga, Tenn.

CHATTANOOGA, TENNESSEE, July 17, 1918. The Florida monument at Chickamauga Battlefield. Printed on back of card: *Dedicated in 1913 during the reunion of the United Confederate Veterans. Florida was represented by seven organizations and four guns in the Battle of Chickamauga.*

AUBURN, ALABAMA, ca. 1903. (Opposite page) A postcard to a Miss Allison in Gurley, Alabama. The writer signs by initials only — T.H.E. He or she is a student at this college, founded by the Methodists in 1857 and named Eastern Alabama Male College. In 1872, it was renamed Alabama Agricultural & Mechanical College, and in 1899 it became Alabama Polytechnic Institute. In 1960, it acquired the name by which all southerners know it today: *Auburn University.* This view is of Samford Hall, the main administration building, built in 1889.

Spanish moss, artfully draping live oak trees in South Carolina (top) and Florida (bottom). Both postcards were published about 1916.

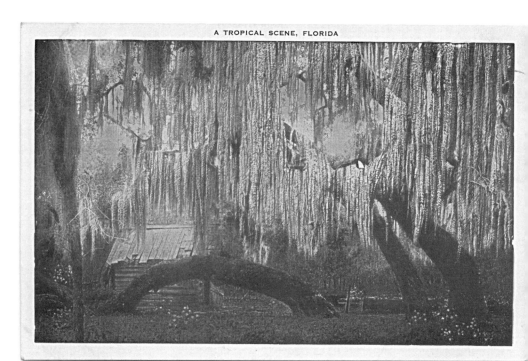

A TROPICAL SCENE, FLORIDA

Beautiful Drive along the Dixie Highway, Florida.

Beautiful and graceful, Spanish moss shrouds two roads in Florida. The view at the top of the page dates back to 1916, while the bottom picture is of 1930s vintage.

"Lovers Lane" in Florida

Cooke County Court House, Gainesville, Texas

33102-N

GAINESVILLE, TEXAS, ca. 1916. The Cooke County Courthouse is a good example of the massive, impressive courthouses that dot the Lone Star state. And, like many a courthouse lawn, this one is graced by an imposing monument to the glorious Confederate dead.

Grand Drive, Forest Park, St. Louis, Mo.

*Cotton Pickers, Homeward Bound.*

Cotton was produced in every state in Dixie. The pictures on these two pages date back to about 1909. (Courtesy Scott Smith)

Hauling Cotton to Market.

NEW ORLEANS, LOUISIANA, November 14, 1916. The Old French Market in its new building, constructed in 1913. The first building, constructed in 1791, was destroyed by a hurricane. A woman from the north, traveling quite extensively, has written back to her mother. "Just a card to say I'm well. . .Horribly dusty here — no rain since August — and warm. Everybody wearing white and sitting outdoors."

D'Evereux, Natchez, Miss.

6A49-N

SAN ANTONIO, TEXAS, ca. 1910. Henry Kubik, Gail Kubik, Mattie Thompson, and Eva Kubik. This family from northeastern Oklahoma is obviously touring San Antonio, where they have decided to take a family portrait in one of those delightful old fake backdrops. Eva is the daughter of Mattie and was an operatic singer of the day.

NATCHEZ, MISSISSIPPI, ca. 1930. (Opposite page). *D'Evereux*, built in 1840, played reluctant host to unwelcome Yankee troops during the War for Southern Independence. Camping on the estate, northern soldiers destroyed the lovely gardens, terraces, lakes, and swans.

HOT SPRINGS, ARKANSAS, January 23, 1913. A view of the bustling little city built upon the reputation of its famous hot mineral springs. This is Central Avenue, looking north.

NATCHEZ, MISSISSIPPI, ca. 1930. *Dunleith*, built in 1856, is the most imposing mansion in Natchez, situated as it is on 40 acres and framed by an ornate iron fence.

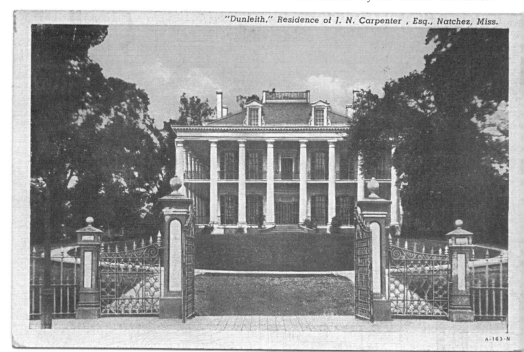

765. MONTICELLO, HOME OF THOMAS JEFFERSON, NEAR CHARLOTTESVILLE, VA.

CHARLOTTESVILLE, VIRGINIA, October 23, 1916. Showing Thomas Jefferson's home, *Monticello*, near Charlottesville, this card was published by the J.P. Bell Company in Lynchburg.

HOUSTON, TEXAS, February 20, 1911. The Carnegie Library and the First Presbyterian Church. By the time of this card, the South, having arisen out of the ashes of War, was a veritable showcase of Victorian architecture.

The Carnegie Library and First Presbyterian Church, Houston, Texas.

ATLANTA, GEORGIA, October 24, 1918. This card was mailed by a traveler in Greenville, South Carolina, to Mrs. W.A. Felts in Kevil, Kentucky. Terminal Station, shown here, was one of the largest in the South and was served by eighty-six passenger trains daily!

3 ST. AUGUSTINE – SLAVE MARKET

*Our Cadet still in St. Augustine will leave in a few days for Jacksonville as ever M. Whitley March 5th 1907*

NATCHEZ, MISSISSIPPI, ca. 1931. This picture of *Longwood* is thought to have been made in 1895. Unfinished when war broke out in 1861, the house remains as it was, the top floors only empty shells with carpenters' tools lying where they left them. The builder, a northern man, left the South at the outbreak of war. (Courtesy Elmore Greaves)


ST. AUGUSTINE, FLORIDA, March 5, 1907. (Opposite page) An old slave market — where employer met employee. Contrary to inflamed imaginations of modern propagandists, the slave market — necessary as it was — was not a place of torture, nor was it an opportunity for splitting up families. Plantation owners understood family ties better than most and bought in family units where they existed.

*This place is only two miles from the place on the postal I sent Harwood. Root for me at ball game. H.D.*

After the War, Mrs. Sarah Dorsey made this Biloxi home available to Jefferson Davis. Here, at *Beauvoir*, he wrote *The Rise and Fall of the Confederate Government* and lived out the rest of his life. In 1902, Mrs. Davis sold the home to the Sons of Confederate Veterans, who allowed the state of Mississippi to begin using it as a home for Confederate soldiers in 1904. In 1940, the SCV began a restoration of the place, opening it as a shrine in 1941. The photograph at the top was made in 1901, while the bottom picture, showing some of the veterans, was made sometime between 1904 and 1911.

Home of Confederate Soldiers, Beauvoir, Miss.

AUSTIN, TEXAS, ca. 1916. The state capitol of Texas was built between 1882 and 1888. Constructed entirely of red granite from quarries at Marble Falls, Texas, it was the second largest public building in the nation when this photograph was taken sometime around 1910. The U.S. capitol in Washington, D.C. was the largest. This card was published by Seawall Specialty Company of Galveston.

SHAWNEE, OKLAHOMA, July 14, 1910. The Baptist Church.

Baptist Church, Shawnee, Okla.

GROVE AVENUE, LOOKING EAST, RICHMOND, VA.

RICHMOND, VIRGINIA, ca. 1916. The architecture of old Richmond is without match. Even today, after urban renewal and corporate greed have exacted their heavy toll, the city has miles of Victorian gems. These row houses on Grove Avenue, like those that line the famous Monument Avenue, are richly embellished with white columns and balustrades, so distinctively Richmond.

12015

UNIVERSITY OF CHATTANOOGA,
CHATTANOOGA, TENN.

Commercial Place and Confederate Monument, Norfolk, Va.

6669

NORFOLK, VIRGINIA, ca. 1908. Printed by the Chessler Company of Baltimore, this card carries the following description: *This splendid tribute to the soldiers of the Confederacy stands in the heart of the retail business section, at the junction of Commercial Place and Main Street, Norfolk.*

CHATTANOOGA, TENNESSEE, July 4, 1909. (Opposite page) This Victorian masterpiece was part of the University of Chattanooga, founded in 1886 as a private, church-sponsored school. In 1969, it became part of the University of Tennessee system. Mrs. Pearl Lusk, of Monterey, Tennessee, received this postcard from a friend. "We are at Chattanooga this a.m. Waiting for hash. Going home today, soon as we see the town. Write soon. Lots of mosquitoes and frogs here. Bad place to live. Come soon."

NEW ORLEANS, LOUISIANA, ca. 1916. (Next page) General Beauregard's residence in the French Quarter as viewed from the opposite direction. The general lived here during the winter of 1866-1867.

GENERAL BEAUREGARD' RESIDENCE, NEW ORLEANS, LA.

9881

NEW ORLEANS, LOUISIANA, December 6, 1923. Mabel sent this postcard of General Pierre Goustave Toutant-Beauregard's residence back to Miss Flora Mai Dodson in Elkton, Tennessee. The Confederate general, a Creole of French descent, was one of few generals to command troops in a broad scope across the South. Among many assignments, he was present at Ft. Sumter, Shiloh, Manassas, and Petersburg.

7022 CHARTRES STREET "VIEUX CARRE" NEW ORLEANS, LA.                    COPR. DETROIT PHOTOGRAPHIC CO.

HENRY CLAY INN, ASHLAND, VIRGINIA                    57174-C

ASHLAND, VIRGINIA, ca. 1916. An architectural gem of perfect symmetry, the Henry Clay Inn is described on the reverse side as "a thoroughly up-to-date hotel, open all year."

MARION, SOUTH CAROLINA, November 12, 1912. The Confederate monument stands guard over one of the beautiful streets in Marion. The extra space at the right end of the card is a leftover of the pre-1907 era when the message had to be written on the front.

Confederate Monument, Marion, S. C.

Gen. Gordon's Home, near ATLANTA, Ga.

*[handwritten message across postcard]*

ATLANTA, GEORGIA, October 29, 1906. *Sutherland*, home of General John B. Gordon, was built on the site of the old home which burned in 1899. It was located in the small community of Kirkwood, four miles from Atlanta. General Gordon served Georgia as both U.S. Senator and Governor after the War. Born in 1832, he died in 1904 and is buried in Oakland Cemetery in Atlanta.

THE OLD MARKET,
CHARLESTON, S. C.—37

Gusher near Tulsa, I. T.

TULSA, INDIAN TERRITORY, April 3, 1908. A familiar sight in the Sooner state, this oil derrick, storage tank, and related buildings were photographed before November 16, 1907, the date of Oklahoma statehood. By the time this card was posted in 1908, the abbreviation "I.T." was already out of date. Like many postcards of that era, this one was printed in Germany.

CHARLESTON, SOUTH CAROLINA, ca. 1918. (Opposite page) Market Hall sits at the head of the historic old market area. In 1788, Charles Cotesworth Pinckney ceded the land to the city, stipulating that a public market be built on the site and forever used as a public market. The bottom of this building is still used as a market, and all of the buildings around and behind it for four blocks are full of vendors. The top floor of Market Hall houses the UDC museum. (See page 116 for another photo.)

MINERAL WELLS, TEXAS, ca. 1907. The Piedmont Hotel.

SOMEWHERE IN THE SOUTH, ca. 1930. If the South is characterized by any one thing, it would have to be white columns.

HOUSTON, TEXAS, March 13, 1909. The exquisite architecture of Central Christian Church in Houston.

NATCHEZ, MISSISSIPPI, September 18, 1948. This card showing *Cottage Gardens,* one of the city's lovely ante-bellum homes, was probably printed in the 1930s. Thelma has just arrived in Natchez and writes back to her mother in Hardy, Arkansas. "Lots of cotton and colored folks here."

13537 "FOUR OAKS" OLD PLANTATION HOME.

LOUISIANA, ca. 1907. The perfect stereotype of Deep South plantation architecture, this old mansion was called *Four Oaks* when photographed by the Detroit Publishing Company for postcard use. If it is the same house identified as *Three Oaks* in a 1941 publication called *White Pillars*, it was built in 1840 near the Mississippi River many miles below New Orleans.

16078— Burton
Jefferson *Nov. 8.*
Davis' Home.
White House *many*
of the *friends*
Confederacy, *for*
Montgomery,
Ala *the paper*
It was en-
joyed by all
Mrs. H. told
of your new
home + on
hope you
will soon
be settled
and get to
quilt.
mama is
at home
at last +
all are well
little love
Allie

The Robert E. Lee Hotel, Jackson, Miss.

2124-30

JACKSON, MISSISSIPPI, March 13, 1939. The Robert E. Lee Hotel. The South used to be justifiably proud of her Confederate heritage. This hotel is but one of thousands of public buildings named for southern heroes. Barely discernible in this view is a Confederate flag hanging to the right of the U.S. flag, once a common sight across Dixie. Southerners, to our own embarrassment, have allowed the liberal media, northern demagogues, black power activists, and assorted interlopers to shame us into a public silence.

MONTGOMERY, ALABAMA, November 9, 1906. (Opposite page) The first White House of the Confederacy was occupied from mid-April until late May, 1861, by President Davis and his family. Seen here, it was located at the corner of Lee and Bibb Streets. In 1920, it was moved near the capitol and splendidly restored.

RICHMOND, VIRGINIA, June 1, 1907. Dunlora Academy was founded in 1830 by the Baptists. In 1840, it was chartered as Richmond College and was known by that name when this picture was taken. In 1920, it became part of the University of Richmond.

DANVILLE, VIRGINIA, ca. 1916. Tobacco buyers.

DANVILLE, VA. THE LARGEST LOOSE-LEAF TOBACCO MARKET IN THE WORLD.

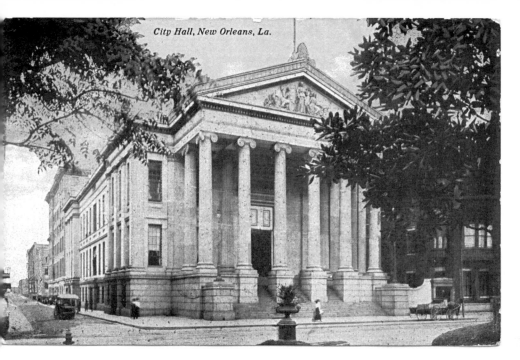

NEW ORLEANS, LOUISIANA, ca. 1907. Here, on December 11, 1889, from the porch of City Hall, was preached the funeral of President Jefferson Davis. These tall columns were draped in black as 200,000 mourners quietly listened, probably unaware that they composed the largest funeral audience the South has ever seen.

LADDONIA, MISSOURI, May, 1908. Family photographs were often made up into postcards. This is J.R. Hodge, astraddle a fine-looking horse.

Central College. CONWAY, Ark.

CONWAY, ARKANSAS, February 2, 1914. Central College was established in 1907 as a teachers' college. In 1967, it became a state college, and in 1975 its name was changed to The University of Central Arkansas.

Arlington Hotel,
Hot Springs National Park, Ark.—18

GORDON MONUMENT, ATLANTA, GA.

ATLANTA, GEORGIA, February 15, 1910. Mailed from Emerson, Georgia, this card reveals the importance attached to the heroes of the Confederacy. General John B. Gordon, Georgia's premier Confederate hero, was one of the officers with Lee at the tragic end in Appomattox.

HOT SPRINGS, ARKANSAS, ca. 1912. (Opposite page) The Arlington Hotel has always been a popular spot for visitors to Hot Springs. This beautiful structure is the second building, and, like the first one, it was destroyed by fire. The third building was constructed in the 1920s and is still a favorite with travelers, many of whom take advantage of the hot mineral baths offered by the hotel.

Old St. John's Church, Broad and 25th Sts., Richmond, Va.

RICHMOND, VIRGINIA, ca. 1916. It was here in Old St. John's Church that Patrick Henry delivered his famous "Give me liberty or give me death" speech to the Virginia Convention in 1775.

ST. PETERSBURG, FLORIDA, February 15, 1926. A concert every day in the old band shell in Williams Park — a St. Petersburg tradition.

St. Petersburg, Florida, The Sunshine City.

Daily Band Concert in Williams Park.

Grammar School Building, Mound City, Mo.

MOUND CITY, MISSOURI, October 3, 1911. For some reason, this card, bearing a picture of the grammar school, was postmarked on the front after it reached its destination of North Platte, Nebraska.

FRANKFORT, KENTUCKY, ca. 1916. The Stewart Home Training School.

Main Building, The Stewart Home Training School, Frankfort, Ky.—12.

Geronimo, Famous Apache War Chief.
(Prisoner of War at Ft. Sill)    (Copyrighted)

OKLAHOMA CITY, OKLAHOMA, 1908. (Opposite page) Ligru Hess mailed this card to his cousin, George Nuessli, in Rock Island, Illinois. He mentions that he is going on to Denver, but he doesn't "like to mouff around all the time." On February 7, 1910, he writes another postcard from Oklahoma City to his cousin, Eurilie Nuessli, saying, "We are down here in the sunny southwest since two weeks. Work is plenty here. Ernst has a job, too. We have some fine weather here." This northerner was still fascinated by Geronimo, for on his second "mouff" into Oklahoma he sends a postcard almost identical to his first, the only exception being that the photograph is raised, or embossed, and the colors are a little brighter. This pose of Geronimo was taken at the post in 1905.

LAWTON, OKLAHOMA, ca. 1907. (Opposite page) Geronimo was one of the most popular subjects of postcards of the Southwest. The most famous of the Apache war chiefs, he resisted the encroachment of the western settlers until his capture in Arizona in 1887. Along with 407 men, women, and children, he was sent to Fort Sill, Oklahoma Territory, then on to Marion Military Prison in St. Augustine, Florida. In 1888, they were moved to Mt. Vernon Barracks in Alabama, where tuberculosis ravaged the pitiful little tribe. In 1894, the 296 survivors were sent back to Fort Sill, where they were settled on the Kiowa-Comanche Reservation. They were held there as Prisoners-of-War until 1913. Geronimo died in captivity in 1909 at the age of 80 and lies buried today in the old cemetery at Fort Sill. Visitors can still visit the old jail where he was held and view the blood-stained floor of his cell. Northerners, whose soldiers had committed the bloodiest of massacres during and after the War Between the States, were especially intrigued with the fierce, independent Indian leaders. This particular postcard was addressed to R.K. Parkhurst of Fairfield, Illinois. His daughter, May, writes, "This old customer has 600 scalps and more to his credit."

INDIANS UP TO DATE. APACHE CHIEF GERONIMO AND THREE BRAVES, OKLAHOMA.

Georgia State Capitol.

ATLANTA, GEORGIA, 1918. The carpetbag government moved the capital from Milledgeville to Atlanta in 1868. After Georgians succeeded in clearing the state of carpetbaggers, this impressive capitol was constructed. Finished in 1889, the dome is overlaid with gold from the mines of north Georgia.

ATLANTA, GEORGIA, December 31, 1919. The Governor's Mansion.

GOVERNOR'S MANSION, ATLANTA, GA.

THE OLD WAR ENGINE AT FORT WALKER. GRANT PARK, ATLANTA, GA.

ATLANTA, GEORGIA, 1918. This old engine, the *Texas,* was used during the War. It is located in Grant Park, a recreational area created from 100 acres given by local citizen L.P. Grant in 1883.

ATLANTA, GEORGIA, 1918. The Sleeping Lion statue. Around this monument in Oakland Cemetery are buried approximately 4,000 Confederate soldiers killed at the Battle of Atlanta. Most of them are unknown, and no one knows for sure just how many are buried here.

Monument to the Unknown Confederate Dead.

HOT SPRINGS, ARKANSAS, July 23, 1920. This postcard of the U.S. Army and Navy Hospital probably dates back to about 1910, and the actual photograph used was probably taken about 1905. In 1920, Miss Lucy R. Groom of Woodbury, Tennessee, received this one from her mother, telling her that her father was about well.

PELHAM'S MONUMENT.    JACKSONVILLE, ALABAMA.

JACKSONVILLE, ALABAMA, April 8, 1923. This view of Major Pelham's monument was sent from a local resident (whose name is illegible) to the Missess Claybrooke in Nashville, Tennessee. On the front, she notes that this impressive statue was erected by the General John H. Forney Chapter of the UDC. John Pelham's death at Kelly's Ford, Virginia, on March 17, 1863, was especially tragic due to his youthful devotion to the cause. Known as "the Boy Major," he had early distinguished himself with the artillery, and at Fredericksburg he held off 24 enemy guns with only two cannons of his own. Eventually down to one, he withdrew only after running out of ammunition. General Lee remarked, "It is glorious to see such courage in one so young."

COLLEGE PARK, GEORGIA, 1918. (Opposite page) Georgia Military Academy opened here in 1900. Built in 1895, this structure was first occupied by Southern Military Academy.

SAN ANTONIO, TEXAS, February 27, 1926. Reminiscent of Florida, San Antonio's Spanish architecture adds an interesting dimension to the South. Shown here are two railroad depots, the M. K. & T., above, and the Southern Pacific, below.

Science Hall, Wofford College, Spartanburg, S. C.

54-10

SPARTANBURG, SOUTH CAROLINA, ca. 1907. Beautiful vine-covered Science Hall at Wofford College.

SPARTANBURG, SOUTH CAROLINA, ca. 1916. Wofford College was established in 1854 by the Methodists.

WOFFORD COLLEGE, SPARTANBURG, S. C.

114397-N

NATCHEZ, MISSISSIPPI, ca. 1930. *Homewood*, built in 1855 by David Hunt, a wealthy man known as the largest slaveholder in America. It was five years under construction and contained a million bricks when finished. This magnificent showplace, with its mahogany fan-spread stairway and silver door knobs, burned to the ground almost 100 years later.

The Conservatory, Kidd Key College, Sherman, Texas.

Court House, Gadsden, Ala.—12

GADSDEN, ALABAMA, ca. 1916. The Etowah County Courthouse is a fine example of Alabama architecture during the 1880s and 1890s. The versatility of red brick lent itself to the ornate, varied styles of the Victorian era.

SHERMAN, TEXAS, ca. 1909. (Opposite page) Kidd-Key College, a finishing school for young ladies, was chartered in 1875 by the Methodist Episcopal Church South as North Texas Female College. In 1919, it was rechartered as a junior college and music conservatory. At some point, it was renamed in honor of Lucy Ann Kidd-Key who served as school president from 1888 until 1916. Many a young lady from the Indian Territory, just north of the Red River, finished up at Kidd-Key. When the school closed in 1937, this magnificent building was bought by the city for use as office space. The city is named for Gen. Sidney Sherman of the Republic of Texas.

205

WEATHERFORD, TEXAS, ca. 1916. Weatherford's most imposing structure is a literal castle on the plains. Built in 1907 to serve as a school and home for the Knights of Pythias, it was designed in the style of a French castle by architect Charles Page.

ALEXANDRIA, LOUISIANA, ca. 1930. City Hall and the Confederate statue.

CITY HALL, ALEXANDRIA, LA.

HOT SPRINGS, ARKANSAS, ca. 1908. This card was published by F.C. Boving of Hot Springs.

TALLAHASSEE, FLORIDA, ca. 1930. This magnificent white-columned home is the Governor's Mansion, a two-story frame house in the gracious Southern Colonial style. It was built in 1908.

PRINGLE HOUSE, CHARLESTON, S. C.

CHARLESTON, SOUTH CAROLINA, ca. 1916. This stately old home has had the dishonor of being occupied by two enemy forces during its long life. In 1780, the British made their headquarters here, and in 1864 the Yankees commandeered the house for the same purpose. Postcard published by the J.S. Pinkussohn Cigar Company of Charleston.

Richmond, Va. Rotunda. The Jefferson Hotel.

General John H. Morgan Monument, Lexington, Ky.

LEXINGTON, KENTUCKY, ca. 1912. The great equestrian statue of Confederate General John Hunt Morgan on the courthouse lawn. Ten thousand people attended the dedication in 1911. A true cavalier, this daring cavalryman was often called "The Thunderbolt of the Confederacy."

RICHMOND, VIRGINIA, May 11, 1909. (Opposite page) The rotunda of the Jefferson Hotel, with its marble statue of Thomas Jefferson. Built in the 1890s, the Jefferson nearly slipped into oblivion in the 1980s. Closed and deteriorating from neglect, it nevertheless received a reprieve when investors restored and reopened the elaborate hotel.

COURT HOUSE AND THE GRAND, MACON, GA.

MACON, GEORGIA, ca. 1916. Published by Evoy Book and Stationery Company, this card shows off some of Macon's exquisite architecture.

BILOXI, MISSISSIPPI, October 26, 1923. Published by Bleuer & Son of Biloxi, this Victorian enticement is reminiscent of scenes in a dream.

A BEAUTIFUL HOME ON THE BEACH, BILOXI, MISS.

GAINESVILLE, FLORIDA, ca. 1920. The First Baptist Church, illustrative of the large, impressive places of worship which characterize southern towns.

SUMTER, SOUTH CAROLINA, ca. 1935. The Sumter County Courthouse.

NS-9  SUMTER COUNTY COURT HOUSE, SUMTER, S. C.

E-5697

BUCKSTAFF BATHS, U. S. RESERVATION, HOT SPRINGS NATIONAL PARK, ARK. WRITE FOR INFORMATION    31251

HOT SPRINGS, ARKANSAS, August 14, 1931. A lady named Jude writes to her mother, Mrs. Rachel Walker, at 210 North Madison, Enid, Oklahoma. "It is wonderful here. I like Hot springs. Would like to live here. Hope you are well and fine."

873    OLD PORTERFIELD HOME, AN ANTE BELLUM RESIDENCE, VICKSBURG, MISS.

Confederate Monument, Fort Smith, Ark.

FORT SMITH, ARKANSAS, ca. 1908. No monuments were ever put up with more loving care than those dedicated to the memory of the Confederate soldier. A defeated people, a lost cause, a shattered economy — and yet, tributes such as this cover Dixie like the dew.

VICKSBURG, MISSISSIPPI, March 31, 1945. (Opposite page) The post office got rather carried away with this card, postmarking it on both front and back. This striking old ante-bellum home was the residence of William and Julia Porterfield. Jefferson Davis stayed here while on a visit to Vicksburg. In the 1930s, Mrs. Porterfield, finding it difficult to maintain the house, had the old landmark destroyed.

DAVIS, OKLAHOMA, ca. 1920s. Turner Falls, 77 feet high, is located in the heart of the Arbuckles. Instead of eroding the falls back into the mountain, the water deposits travertine as it rushes over the rocks, building the falls ever outward. (See pages 302-305.)

DAVIS, OKLAHOMA, ca. 1920s. Price's Falls, in the Arbuckle Mountains, six miles south of Davis.

*The grass is green here and the trees hang in masses of moss*

NEW ORLEANS, LOUISIANA, January 26, 1925. This scene in Audubon Park spotlights the familiar and much-loved Spanish moss of the South. Here, it hangs on ancient live oak trees.

SAINT SIMONS ISLAND, GEORGIA, ca. 1916. Although this old Victorian church house was built many years ago, it was not the first one on this site. Christ Church held its first service on February 15, 1736, at this site.

CHRIST CHURCH, FREDERICA, ST. SIMONS ISLAND, BRUNSWICK, GA.

89540

53984-C

ASHEVILLE, NORTH CAROLINA, ca. 1935. The Biltmore Mansion, home of the late George W. Vanderbilt, took five years to build. The largest private home in America, it is now a popular tourist attraction. Vanderbilt was visiting Asheville in 1887 when he was struck with the beauty of the area and decided to build his French chateau there.

**RICHMOND LIGHT INFANTRY BLUES, ARMORY (16TH AND MARSHALL STS.), RICHMOND, VA.**

BM-17 ON THE FRONT VERANDA, ROBERT E. LEE HALL,

BLUE RIDGE ASSEMBLY, BLUE RIDGE, N. C. L-8036

BLUE RIDGE, NORTH CAROLINA, ca. 1930. Blue Ridge Assembly, owned and oper-
ated by the YMCA, is near the town of Black Mountain. This view is from the front
porch of Robert E. Lee Hall.

RICHMOND, VIRGINIA, ca. 1910. (Opposite page) The new armory for the Richmond
Blues. The back of the postcard reads: *One of the oldest and most widely known military
organizations in the U.S. Election to membership is a highly prized honor. Organized May 10,
1789, and except during Reconstruction days — when it was prohibited from so doing — has
borne arms in peace and in war. Mustered into service of the Confederacy in June, 1861.
Served with distinction throughout that conflict and, with a "remnant of 16 survivors," surrendered at Appomattox.* The new armory was dedicated May 10, 1910.

Chartres Street,
View in the Old French Quarter,
New Orleans, La.—101

NEW ORLEANS, LOUISIANA, ca. 1916. Chartres Street, one of the oldest streets in the South, is in the heart of the French Quarter.

CLARKSDALE, MISSISSIPPI, ca. 1930. A beautifully proportioned building, the Baptist Church exemplifies southern architecture of the early 20th century.

Baptist Church, Clarksdale, Miss.

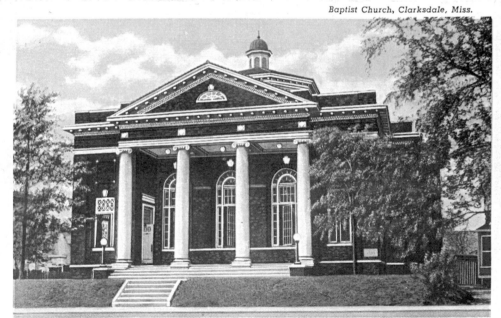

8A473-N

Confederate Rest., Mobile, Ala.

MOBILE, ALABAMA, ca. 1907. Confederate Rest, situated in the southeast corner of Magnolia Cemetery, contains the remains of 1200 Confederate soldiers neatly buried around this sacred monument to the Confederate dead.

NORFOLK, VIRGINIA, ca. 1916. The U.S. Customs House stands like a Greek temple in this old photo of Main Street.

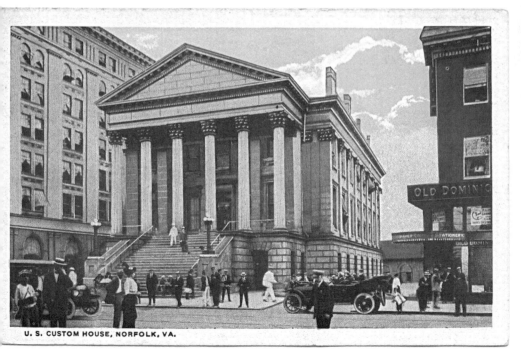

U. S. CUSTOM HOUSE, NORFOLK, VA.

Dans-le' Mer and Breakers Casino, Palm Beach, Florida.

PALM BEACH, FLORIDA, April 2, 1926. One of those famous old oceanside play-grounds of white sand, blue water, and boardwalks. Small wonder Florida has become a retirement mecca. Scenes like this have forever drawn inlanders southward.

Peachtree Street North from Grand Opera House, Atlanta, Ga.

215143

Confederate Monument, Jackson, Miss.

A292

JACKSON, MISSISSIPPI, August 24, 1910. Mailed from Jackson by George Peterson to his friend in Port Gibson, this postcard features the Confederate monument south of the old state capitol. The photograph may have been made on June 4, 1891, when the monument was dedicated, or in some later year at Confederate Memorial Day ceremonies. The base of the enormous statue is draped with Confederate Battle Flags, while park benches and a speaker's stand can be seen to the right.

ATLANTA, GEORGIA, March 6, 1912. (Opposite page) Looking north on Peachtree Street in the old city of Atlanta.

221

EAST BATTERY, CHARLESTON, S. C.                                      88703

CHARLESTON, SOUTH CAROLINA. These two postcard views possibly date back to 1916 and perhaps a few years earlier. Both photographs show the carefully preserved homes in the historic part of Charleston known as "The Battery."

71718    RESIDENCES ON THE BATTERY, CHARLESTON, S. C.

CHARLESTON, SOUTH CAROLINA. Two more views of The Battery. The upper photo was taken in 1904, while the lower photograph may have been taken about 1910.

The Baptist University for Women—Raleigh, N.C. Jan 23, 1909.

*This is only one block from Aunt boarding house. Annié*

RALEIGH, NORTH CAROLINA, January 23, 1909. Established in 1889 and chartered as Baptist Female University in 1891, this college was renamed Baptist University for Women in 1905. Not long after this card was mailed in 1909, the school acquired its present name, Meredith College.

Beech St. Baptist Church, Texarkana, Ark.

State House and Confederate Monument, Raleigh, N. C.

217190

RALEIGH, NORTH CAROLINA, November 23, 1919. The majestic Confederate monument seems to dwarf the state capitol from this angle. When this enormous statue was raised, North Carolinians were wonderfully unreconstructed and unrepentant of their attempt to secure independence. On the base of the granite memorial are these words: FIRST AT SUMTER — LAST AT APPOMATTOX.

TEXARKANA, ARKANSAS, August 20, 1907. (Opposite page) Beech Street Baptist Church. When structures like this were designed and constructed, building was an art. Today it is merely an enterprise.

4A-H1215

BRADENTON, FLORIDA, January 29, 1939. Postcards like this are the reason so many people flocked to Florida. Who could resist a scene like this?

RICHMOND, VIRGINIA, ca. 1916. The Cathedral of the Sacred Heart was consecrated in 1906. Upon its architrave, graven in stone, are the words of our Lord: *IF YE LOVE ME, KEEP MY COMMANDMENTS.*

CATHEDRAL OF THE SACRED HEART (LAUREL STREET), RICHMOND, VA.

HOT SPRINGS, ARKANSAS, June 21, 1912. Central Avenue, the main thoroughfare in this picturesque town.

RICHMOND, VIRGINIA, ca. 1916. The heroic-size statue of Stonewall Jackson on Richmond's famed Monument Avenue. The beloved Jackson, Lee's right hand, died from a wound on May 10, 1863, plunging the South into deepest mourning.

RIDGECREST, NORTH CAROLINA, ca. 1938. Two views of Pritchell Hall, one of the imposing structures at Ridgecrest Baptist Assembly, located in the beautiful Blue Ridge Mountains east of Asheville.

# POST CARD

RIDGECREST, NORTH CAROLINA, ca. 1935. Rhododendron Hall is one of the handsome buildings at the Ridgecrest Baptist Assembly grounds, an 1100-acre summer retreat of the Southern Baptists.

*Residence of Mrs. H. M. King, Corpus Christi, Tex.*

CORPUS CHRISTI, TEXAS, ca. 1908. The residence of Mrs. H.M. King was built about 1882 on what is called "The Bluff," a residential area overlooking the ocean. This Victorian masterpiece was demolished to make way for a Presbyterian church.

ATLANTA, GEORGIA, September 23, 1909. The First Christian Church.

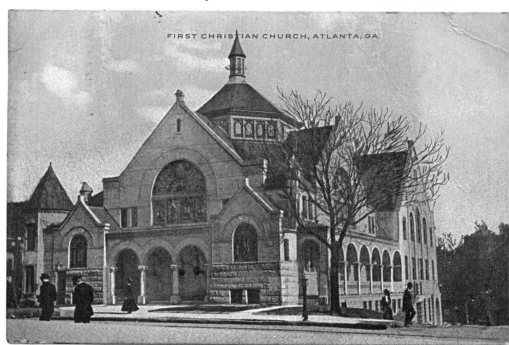

FIRST CHRISTIAN CHURCH, ATLANTA, GA.

62518

LAKE CHARLES, LOUISIANA, ca. 1930. A splendid view of the courthouse of Calcasieu Parish.


WILSON, NORTH CAROLINA, ca. 1920. Bidding on tobacco in a tobacco warehouse.

55786

INTERIOR OF A LOOSE LEAF TOBACCO WAREHOUSE, WILSON, N. C.
THE LARGEST BRIGHT LEAF MARKET IN THE WORLD.

GREETINGS FROM STROUD, OKLA.

SA-H1011

STROUD, OKLAHOMA, ca. 1930. One of many oil fields in the Sooner state. The first well came in the same year as the famous Titusville well in Pennsylvania (1859) but it was around the turn of the century that the boom occurred. Almost overnight towns sprang up around newly discovered pools, earning the not-so-salubrious sobriquet of "boom towns."

J. A. BUCHANAN RESIDENCE, TEXARKANA, ARK.

E 9756 LEE MONUMENT, RICHMOND, VA.

RICHMOND, VIRGINIA, July 26, 1909. The cornerstone for the great equestrian statue of Lee was laid October 27, 1887. Designed by Antonin Mercié, the monument was dedicated May 29, 1890.

TEXARKANA, ARKANSAS, ca. 1916. (Opposite page) This sprawling mansion, the home of J.A. Buchanan, was probably only a few years old when this photograph was taken. One of the new homes of the period, it was considered quite modern and up-to-date.

CITY HALL, NORFOLK, VA.

NORFOLK, VIRGINIA, ca. 1916. City Hall with its lovely park and fountain.

LAURENS, SOUTH CAROLINA, ca. 1916. The Methodist Church.

FIRST M. E. CHURCH SOUTH, LAURENS, S. C.

COURT HOUSE, JACKSONVILLE. FLA.

JACKSONVILLE, FLORIDA, ca. 1916. The Duval County Courthouse.

NATCHEZ, MISSISSIPPI, ca. 1920. *Green Leaves*, built prior to the War of 1812, is surrounded by age old live oaks.

GREEN LEAVES, NATCHEZ, MISS.

*Metairie cemetery New Orleans.*

NEW ORLEANS, LOUISIANA, 1901. Tombs in Metairie Cemetery. Note cast iron lawn furniture in front of several vaults. President Davis was buried in this cemetery on December 11, 1889, and later moved to Hollywood Cemetery in Richmond. The photograph for this postcard was made and copyrighted in 1900.

Old St. Louis Cemetery, New Orleans, La.

20848

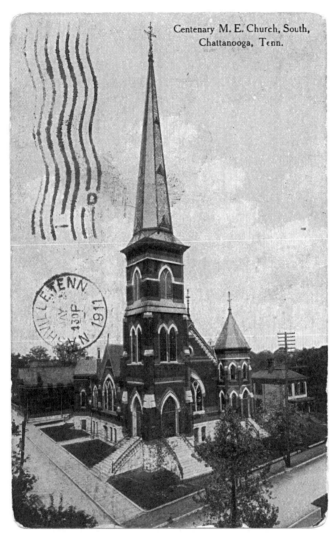

Centenary M. E. Church, South,
Chattanooga, Tenn.

CHATTANOOGA, TENNESSEE, May 2, 1911. This postcard showing the Centenary Methodist Church was postmarked on the back at 11:30 a.m. in Chattanooga. It was postmarked again, this time on the front, when it arrived in Nashville at 1:30 p.m. — the same day! This was before air mail, zip codes, affirmative action, and quotas.

NEW ORLEANS, LOUISIANA, ca. 1916. (Opposite page) Here in the old St. Louis Cemetery, the burying is done above ground. The vaults on the left comprise the seven-foot wall surrounding the cemetery, and the poorer classes are buried therein. Note the tombs of the wealthier class on the right.

George Washington Equestrian Monument, Richmond, Va.

RICHMOND, VIRGINIA, ca. 1916. The Washington Monument against the backdrop of Richmond's Victorian-style City Hall.

NEW ORLEANS, LOUISIANA, ca. 1907. Architecture doesn't get much better than this, the home of W.T. Jay, on Audubon Place. The card was published by C.B. Mason of New Orleans.

Residence Of W. T. Jay. Audibon Place. New Orleans, La.

MOWBRAY ARCH. NORFOLK. VA.

NORFOLK, VIRGINIA, ca. 1916. This Victorian view of beautiful Norfolk was published by the Nowitzky News Company of that city.

NEW ORLEANS, LOUISIANA, March 8, 1916. A cool, inviting view of the lush foliage surrounding this white-columned porch and its tree-shaded yard.

FOLIAGE ABOUT A NEW ORLEANS, LA. RESIDENCE.

NEW ORLEANS, LOUISIANA, March 11, 1911. One of the beautiful homes on St. Charles Avenue. This card, published by F.M. Kirby of New Orleans, was mailed by Mrs. L.D. Webb to her friend, Miss Watson Tullis, of Alexandria, Louisiana.

LAUREL, MISSISSIPPI, April 14, 1914. An extraordinarily handsome monument to the beloved Confederate soldier.

CHARLESTON, SOUTH CAROLINA, ca. 1916. (Opposite page) Henry Timrod's famous ode was written for the Confederate decoration service here in Magnolia Cemetery in 1867. Its last stanza has found its way onto many a Confederate monument throughout Dixie.

> Stoop angels, hither from the skies,
>> There is no holier spot of ground
> Than where defeated valor lies,
>> By mourning beauty crowned!

241

Cotton Compress, Oklahoma, Okla.

RICHMOND, VIRGINIA, ca. 1916. (Opposite page) The tomb of Jefferson Davis in Hollywood Cemetery.

Confederate Museum, White House of the Confederacy and Jeff. Davis Mansion, Richmond, Va.

OKLAHOMA CITY, OKLAHOMA, May 27, 1909. (Opposite page) Like the rest of the South, Oklahoma produced an abundance of cotton. Here, at the compress, 500-pound bales are compressed into smaller bales only one-third the size of the original, making it possible to ship more cotton in less space. Cotton was shipped by rail, and any town with a good-sized ginning operation needed a compress. These bales are probably headed for Houston, Galveston, or New Orleans, where they will be exported.

JEFFERSON DAVIS TOMB, HOLLYWOOD CEMETERY, RICHMOND, VA.

RICHMOND, VIRGINIA, ca. 1907. (Opposite page) The White House of the Confederacy. Built in 1818 by Dr. John Brockenbrough, it was bought by the city of Richmond and offered to President Davis, who chose to lease the property upon his arrival in 1861. Varina Davis commented upon her new home. "In July we moved to the old Brockenbrough house, and began to feel somewhat more at home when walking through the old-fashioned terraced garden or the large airy rooms. . . . The mansion stands on the brow of a steep and very high hill. . . . The house is very large, but the rooms are comparatively few, as some of them are over forty feet square. The ceilings are high, the windows wide, and the well-staircases turn in easy curves toward the airy rooms above." Today, the mansion is beautifully restored to reflect the splendor of its four years as Confederate White House, a magnificent tribute to the culture of the South.

NEW STATE CAPITOL, LITTLE ROCK, ARK.

JACKSON, MISSISSIPPI, May 21, 1908. (Opposite page) The new state capitol, pictured here soon after its completion in 1903, shows the dome designed by George Mann.

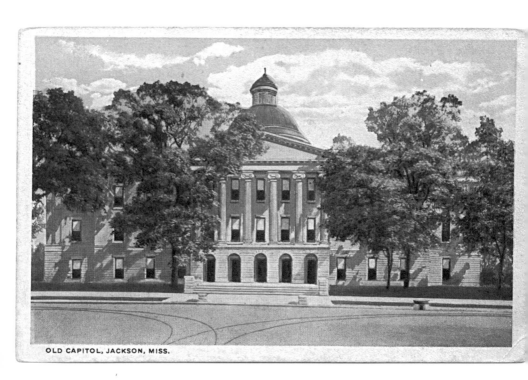

OLD CAPITOL, JACKSON, MISS.

LITTLE ROCK, ARKANSAS, ca. 1908. (Opposite page) Construction of the state capitol began in 1899, under the supervision of architect George Mann. This postcard view, at first thought to be an actual photograph, turned out to be Mann's meticulous architectural drawing. In 1907, Mann was dismissed, leaving the capitol completed except for the dome and a few ornamental details. Cass Gilbert, a New York architect brought in to complete the building, did not like Mann's proposed dome. He insisted on copying the dome from the state capitol in Jackson, Mississippi. Mann got the last laugh, however, for upon completion of Arkansas's dome in 1916, Mann announced that it was he who had designed the dome on the Mississippi state capitol.

State Capitol, Jackson, Miss.

JACKSON, MISSISSIPPI, ca. 1916. (Opposite page) The State House, built in 1839, served as state capitol until 1903 when the government moved into the new and larger capitol a few blocks away. Attempts were made to demolish it, but women's preservation groups obtained a stay of execution, and it was turned into office space in 1916. In 1954, legislators again introduced legislation to destroy the building, but Governor Coleman, in 1959, directed that it be restored to house a state museum. Today, it is a rare gem of Mississippi architecture and is open to the public.

CHURCH OF THE REDEEMER, BILOXI, MISS.

HAMPTON, VIRGINIA, ca. 1916. (Opposite page) Old St. John's Church, cemetery, and monument to the Confederate dead.

State Capitol, Montgomery, Ala.

BILOXI, MISSISSIPPI, ca. 1907. (Opposite page) They do it right in Mississippi! In 1873 and 1874, the Church of the Redeemer was constructed along the Gulf Coast. It was a wooden building, in which Jefferson Davis worshipped regularly until his death in 1889. Six years later, the congregation built the brick church pictured here; however, they did not tear the old church house down. Instead, they simply built in front of it, closer to Beach Boulevard, turning the old structure into a parish hall and church school. Seventy-four years later, in 1969, Hurricane Camille demolished the brick building and, in a strange twist of fate, left the old wooden church standing. It was rehabilitated for worship and now serves the same purpose it served in 1874. The moral of the story? Never tear down your old building. You just might need it again.

Old St. John's Church, Hampton, Va.

MONTGOMERY, ALABAMA, June 1, 1908. (Opposite page) Standing below these graceful columns, Jefferson Davis took the oath of office for the presidency of the Confederate States of America on February 18, 1861. A bronze star marks the historic place where he stood. On this postcard, the white strip on the right end is a leftover from the era when messages had to be written on the front. On March 1, 1907, it became lawful to write both message and address on the back, and even though the back of this card carries the new printing for the "divided back," the front just hadn't caught up with the times!

SOLDIERS' HOME (BOULEVARD AND GROVE AVENUE), RICHMOND, VA.

MISSISSIPPI RIVER, August 19, 1920. (Opposite page) The passenger steamer, *G.W. Hill.*

STATE CAPITOL BUILDING, BATON ROUGE, LA.

RICHMOND, VIRGINIA, ca. 1916. (Opposite page) The central grounds of the Virginia Confederate Soldiers Home. Historical data on the back of the card reads: *Situated in a beautiful grove in the western portion of the City are the comfortable cottages constituting the home maintained by the State for the benefit of native-born Confederate veterans and those who served in Virginia regiments. Here, these honored heroes, "by time subdued," are spending the evening of life, calmly and fearlessly awaiting the inevitable summons to spread their tents on the eternal camping-ground.*

STEAMER G. W. HILL ON MISSISSIPPI RIVER.

BATON ROUGE, LOUISIANA, ca. 1907. (Opposite page) Built in the style of an English castle, the old state capitol particularly annoyed Mark Twain, who wasted much time criticizing its architecture. Calling it a "little sham castle," he blamed the design on Sir Walter Scott, whose novels were widely read when construction began in 1848. In 1862, the Yankees burned it and moved the seat of their oppressive rule to New Orleans. After Reconstruction finally ended, Louisiana rebuilt the capitol from its burned-out shell and made Baton Rouge the capital city again. In 1932, the state government moved into a new building. Louisianans, showing much better taste than either Mark Twain or the Yankees, restored the old capitol as a museum.

FRANKFORT, KENTUCKY, ca. 1910. The new state capitol, completed in 1910.

WESTMORELAND, VIRGINIA, ca. 1916. *Stratford Hall,* ancestral home of the Lees, is the birthplace of the South's greatest hero, Robert E. Lee. Built in 1727 in the English style, *Stratford Hall* sits near the Potomac River.

OCEAN FOREST HOTEL, MYRTLE BEACH, S. C. "AMERICA'S FINEST STRAND"

5A-H1320

MYRTLE BEACH, SOUTH CAROLINA, ca. 1939. A view of the Ocean Forest Hotel.

CROWLEY, LOUISIANA, ca. 1921. The First Methodist Church.

*First Methodist Episcopal Church South, Crowley, La.*

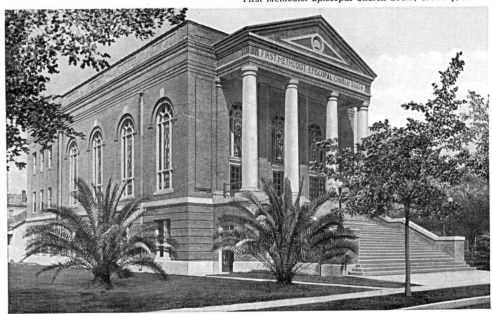

87674

ST. LOUIS, MISSOURI, ca. 1907. St. Louis was the crossroads of America. Union Station was the largest railroad depot in the world.

BEAUFORT, SOUTH CAROLINA, ca. 1907. Advertised as "hand-colored," this postcard showing *The Anchorage* was published by Luther's Pharmacy of Beaufort. (See page 362 for another picture of this home.)

# Post Card

First Baptist Church,
Barnesville, Ga.

BARNESVILLE, GEORGIA, ca. 1930. First Baptist Church.

MERIDIAN, MISSISSIPPI, ca. 1915. The Confederate monument at the Lauderdale County Courthouse.

GREENSBORO, NORTH CAROLINA, September 3, 1909. The Elks' Lodge.

WETUMKA, OKLAHOMA, ca. 1914. Cotton growers lined up around the old bandstand on Main Street.

THE ALCAZAR HOTEL, ST. AUGUSTINE, FLA.

ST. AUGUSTINE, FLORIDA, ca. 1916. The Alcazar Hotel, built in the Spanish Renaissance style by oil magnate Henry Morrison Flagler, opened in late 1888.

OKLAHOMA CITY, OKLAHOMA, August 25, 1914. This architectural diamond, the Carnegie Library, like so much of Oklahoma City's early architecture, is *gone with the wind*.

Carnegie Library, Oklahoma City, Okla.

PLACE STAMP HERE

DOMESTIC ONE CENT

FOREIGN TWO CENTS

SCENE IN BEAUTIFUL GROUNDS OF TAMPA BAY HOTEL, TAMPA, FLA.

TAMPA, FLORIDA, ca. 1916. The Tampa Bay Hotel. Postcard published by Tampa News Company.

WHERE STEPHEN COLLINS FOSTER WROTE "MY OLD KENTUCKY HOME"

BARDSTOWN, KENTUCKY, ca. 1930. The parlor in the home of Stephen Foster's cousin, John Rowan. It was here in 1852 that Foster wrote *My Old Kentucky Home,* one of his many plantation melodies.

BARDSTOWN, KENTUCKY, ca. 1930. Mrs. Rowan's bedroom in the mansion.

*Mrs. Rowan's Bedroom*

7A451-N

*"Federal Hill"* — Where Stephen Collins Foster Wrote His Immortal Song *"My Old Kentucky Home"*

BARDSTOWN, KENTUCKY, ca. 1930. An exterior view of *Federal Hill*, where Stephen Foster wrote his popular song. Judge John Rowan built the house in 1795 with bricks brought over from England. They arrived at Newport News, Virginia, and were transported by oxen-drawn sleds over Indian trails to Kentucky.

THIS SIDE FOR THE ADDRESS

ARTISTIC

PHOTOGRAPHY

W. E. SINGLETON,
257 GAY STREET,
KNOXVILLE. ▲ ▲ ▲ TENN.

Duplicates at Reduced prices.
View work a Specialty.

# PART THREE

NASHVILLE, TENNESSEE, ca. 1870. (Opposite page) The children of Robert and Elizabeth Herbert, about five years after the end of the War. All of the boys served in the Confederate army except Thomas, who was only a child at the time. George enlistd at the age of 13$^1/_2$. Standing on the back row are: Thomas L. Herbert, George Washington Sneed Herbert (Co. G, 8th Texas Cavalry), David Cummings Herbert (Co. B, 11th Tennessee Cavalry), and Robert N. Herbert (Co. B, 20th Tennessee Infantry). Seated are: James Harvey Herbert (Co. I, 4th Texas Infantry), Mary Elizabeth Herbert Carmichael, and John O. Herbert (Co. B, 20th Tennessee Infantry).

David was in Gen. Nathan Bedford Forrest's command, while James served in Gen. John Bell Hood's brigade. Young George, who was in the celebrated Texas Rangers, was later transferred to the famous Coleman's Scouts where he saw duty with Sam Davis and DeWitt Smith Jobe. He never surrendered and never took a loyalty oath.

NASHVILLE, TENNESSEE, ca. 1903. (Opposite page) The same family, thirty-three years later. George, James, David, Mary, Thomas, and Robert. Absent from this picture is John, who had passed away in 1871 at the age of thirty-four. The four veterans are here shown wearing badges and medals commemorating their unselfish service to the South during the War for Southern Independence.

STEELE, ALABAMA, 1880. A unique photograph, this depicts an early gathering of Confederate veterans, eight years before the United Confederate Veterans was organized. Unlike most of the later reunion photos, this one reveals youthful faces. Some of these veterans are apparently still in their 30s and 40s, and only a few have that aged look to which we are accustomed in the more numerous reunion photographs of a later era. (Courtesy Hunter Phillips)

TULLAHOMA, TENNESSEE, ca. 1912. The Coke wagon on a snowy winter day. The boxes in the back of the truck are labeled: *Coca Cola Bottling Works, McMinnville, Tenn.* (Courtesy Edwin P'Pool)

SULPHUR SPRINGS, ALABAMA, August 7, 1924. A reunion of Confederate veterans. (Courtesy David Hammock)

HILLSBORO, TEXAS, ca. 1893. Made in the Bunnell Studio, located at 78¹/₂ West Side Square.

NASHVILLE, TENNESSEE, August 11, 1907. (Opposite page) Opening day for The Dixie, an early theater in Nashville. The admission price was only 5¢, and one can bet that the entertainment offered was more wholesome, enjoyable, and entertaining than what $6.00 will buy today. (Courtesy Edwin P'Pool)

4254—
Washington
Tomb, Mt.
Vernon, Va

MOUNT VERNON, VIRGINIA, ca. 1901. From a postcard, this is a view of the tomb of George Washington and his wife, Martha.

WYNNEWOOD, INDIAN TERRITORY, ca. 1900. (Opposite page) A school picture, taken on a cold winter day. On March 14, 1933, Earl Crump, who was about ten years old in this photograph, sat down and identified all but one person, the little boy at the upper left end, his face obscured by a damage spot. There also appears to be an unidentified person barely visible inside the doorway.

(Bottom row) Lewis Cock, Earl Crump, Will Cock, Howard Eskridge, Perry Howeth, Harry Moore, Jim Jennings.

(Second row) John Howeth, Pierce Cochran, Claude Nisler, Emma Taylor, Lucile Roberts, Gussie Smith, Eula Cochran, Dean Haley, Naomi Sells, Myrtle Haley, Mae West (?).

The two boys sitting at the left, behind the second row are Jess Riggan and Jep Knight.

(Third row) Unidentified boy, Jim Dougherty, John McMillan, Mildred Moore, Ida Belle Schmidt, Julia Herring, Bessie Roberts, Malissa Kellar, Jessie Lawrence, Grace Mackey, Bonnie Carr, Lillian Rabb.

(Fourth row) Ruth Sells, Acca Walner, Lula Jennings, Julia Walner, Susie Lawrence, Clifford Secrest, Ollie Scott.

(Top row) Miss Taylor, Mrs. Burwell, Kate Daugherty, Kate Kendall, Icy White, Allie Macky.

TEXAS, ca. 1912. Captain James T. Hunter, a veteran of Company H, 4th Texas Infantry, is shown here wearing his Southern Cross of Honor. (Courtesy Ben S. Grimland and Edwina Hunter Burkhalter)

DURHAM, NORTH CAROLINA, ca. 1888. The Victorian home of E.J. Parrish.

DE LEON SPRINGS, FLORIDA, ca. 1890. Florida — nature's playground. Warm weather, Spanish moss, live oaks, clear water, and the luxury of a lazy afternoon.

DENTON, TEXAS, ca. 1895. "A Baptist minister, Rev. Hearod." That's the message, scrawled on the back of this well-preserved photograph which was made in the Williams Studio in Denton.

SHREVEPORT, LOUISIANA, June, 1865. A rare find, this is believed to be the last Confederate photograph of the War. On May 26, 1865, General Buckner, at that time in New Orleans and acting for Gen. E. Kirby Smith, accepted terms for surrendering the forces of the Trans-Mississippi Department. On June 2, General Smith approved the terms from Galveston, terms which immediately paroled soldiers and officers and freed them to go home. Wishing to record for posterity a remembrance of their gallant efforts and long association with the Confederate cause, these officers gathered in Shreveport for the last photograph, donning clean, unused uniforms which were probably carefully preserved in anticipation of celebrating a Confederate victory rather than the loss that brought them to this Shreveport studio. Standing, from left to right are William Freret; unidentified man; D.C. Proctor, First Louisiana Engineers; and David French Boyd, Major of Engineers. Seated are Octave Hopkins, First Louisiana Engineers; H.T. Douglas, Colonel of Engineers; and Richard M. Venable. (Courtesy University of the South)

NASHVILLE, TENNESSEE, 1903. While attending the last reunion of Confederate generals, Gen. Fitzhugh Lee (left) and Gen. William Hicks Jackson (right) were photographed at General Jackson's home, *Belle Meade.*

PAULS VALLEY, INDIAN TERRITORY, 1904. "Tom Thumb Weddings" were popular around the turn of the century. This elaborate mock wedding was a pageant of thirty-three girls and twelve boys. The couple who "got married," Warren Gibson and Berniece Kendall, are standing in the center on the first row. To Warren's left are Ance Carroll and Catheryn Witten. To the right of Berniece is Marian Allender. Marie Robinson is also in this photograph, possibly to the right of Marian. The groom was all of four years old. (Courtesy Adrienne Grimmett)

DEWEY COUNTY, OKLAHOMA TERRITORY, ca. 1900. (Opposite page) This sun-drenched scene occurred at a creek near the town of Leedey, where a baptizin' was taking place. The baptismal candidates are in the water near the center of the picture. One of them — the girl who has her head cocked to one side — is Beulah Mae Carter. The preacher stands on the bank, just to the left of the group, and is holding what appears to be a Bible. Beulah's parents stand in the foreground, her mother dressed in dark clothes and looking this way. Her father, James Marion Carter, stands next to his wife, Fanny, and holds something under his arm. The Carters, who were Baptists, had moved to the territory during the 1890s from Henry County, Tennessee, in order to homestead property in the newly opened Cheyenne-Arapaho lands. Like the major-ity of immigrants into what would become the state of Oklahoma in 1907, James Carter was a Confederate veteran, having served in Co. K, 10th Tennessee Cavalry. (Courtesy Stephen L. Carter)

VIRGINIA, ca. 1863. General Eppa Hunton was brigadier general of Virginia militia when war broke out in 1861. He took the field as colonel of the 8th Virginia Infantry, subsequently accepting promotion by the Confederacy to brigadier general in 1863. A former school teacher, lawyer, and member of the secession convention, he was equally prominent on the field of battle, leading his forces in most of the important campaigns of the Army of the Potomac. After the War, he represented Virginia in both the House of Representatives and in the Senate, where he was the only southern member of the famed electoral commission which decided the disputed presidential election of 1877. That important decision required removal of federal troops from the South, thus ending the nightmare of Reconstruction.

LANETT, ALABAMA, ca. 1900. Oh, those beautiful babies! Was there ever a baby who grew up unphotographed? This little one posed for the camera of James Y. East.

DURHAM, NORTH CAROLINA, 1888. *Somerset Villa*, a palatial home in the Victorian style.

Co. A of Nashville
Photo by BIN 'HAM
Memphis Oct 6. 1915.

NEW ORLEANS, LOUISIANA, ca. 1908. J.R. Winder, Confederate veteran who served with General Lee until April 8, 1865, the day before Lee's surrender. The road to Lynchburg was still open, and anyone who wanted to get away and join General Johnston's army was encouraged to go before the terms of surrender were made. About 1200 men, including Winder, escaped by that route, reporting on April 17 to General Johnston's headquarters at Greensboro, North Carolina, only to learn that General Johnston would also capitulate. (*Confederate Veteran*, April, 1909)

MEMPHIS, TENNESSEE, October 6, 1915. (Opposite page) The survivors of Company A, a Nashville unit, and their UDC sponsors pose for a reunion photograph in Memphis. (Courtesy Edwin P'Pool)

NASHVILLE, TENNESSEE, ca. 1895.

PAULS VALLEY, OKLAHOMA, ca. 1907. The Masonic Hall was built in 1906, one year before statehood. Meetings were held on one or both of the upstairs floors, while the bottom floor was rented out to an ice cream parlor on the left and the Elite Cafe on the right.

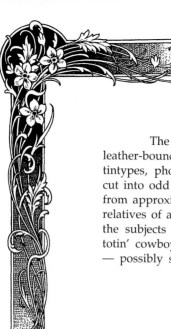

The following pictures, thirteen in all, were found in an old leather-bound album from Richmond, Virginia. The first eleven are tintypes, photographs developed on sensitized pieces of tin, often cut into odd shapes and irregular sizes. These images range in date from approximately 1860 to 1880 and are thought to be friends and relatives of a Richmond resident, though it is evident that not all of the subjects were of the Richmond area. The picture of the gun-totin' cowboys, one of whom is a Mexican, hints of the Southwest — possibly south central or west Texas.

These two images are on *cartes de visites,* or visiting cards. From the same Richmond photo album, they show on their reverse sides the names of the studio, Vannerson & Jones, which was located at "Nos. 188 & 77 Main Street, Richmond, Va." In addition, there is a three-cent revenue stamp affixed to the back of each card, bearing a cancellation similar to the kind used by the post office. Both stamps were cancelled March 26, 1866.

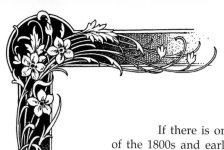

If there is one common thread running through photographs of the 1800s and early 1900s, it is the sober, serious, stern look upon the faces of the people of that era. For whatever reason, it was the custom of the day to look serious and as dignified as possible when having your picture made — a practice most people now find amusing. Today, modern photographers labor to coax exaggerated smiles from their subjects, but one has to ponder what people a hundred years into the future might think about our toothy grins and silly smirks if, by that time, the serious, dignified studio demeanor is once more in vogue.

Even though the look of austerity and solemnity was universal in photography of the last century, and in light of the widely held belief of those of our generation that no one had his picture made "just for the fun of it," it is that much more remarkable and satisfying to find those few exceptions that actually do exist. The following nine photographs amply illustrate the fact that unorthodoxy was not merely a clinical term in the Victorian South.

RICHMOND, VIRGINIA, ca. 1870. Keeping a straight face, this woman departs from propriety in a comic pose. Playing cards was not an activity for a lady, and having her picture made at a card table in a studio was even less acceptable. This tintype may have provided some laughs for her friends.

HOT SPRINGS, ARKANSAS, ca. 1910.

ARDMORE, INDIAN TERRITORY, ca. 1899.

COOPER, TEXAS, ca. 1895. Made in the studio of Miller and Barrett, this photograph advertises W.A. Tyne's Racket Store. Racket stores featured low-priced goods for the home and personal use and were called in more recent times dime stores, five-and-dime, five-and-ten-cent stores, and variety stores. This pretty lady seems to be wearing some of the goods which were probably available at Tyne's — a frivolous hat, inexpensive beads, a bracelet, artificial flowers, a hand bell, a strainer, and an eggbeater! Her chin rests upon a folded fan.

This humorous photograph was made up into a postcard in Harlowton, Montana, and mailed by Bill to J.W. Stewart back home in Bushyhead, Indian Territory, on September 3, 1906. He asks, "Can you find me?"

FORT WORTH, TEXAS, ca. 1899.

FORT WORTH, TEXAS, January 17, 1897. "From Penn to Bob." Penn Rabb, holding the gun, mailed this photograph from Polytechnic College in Fort Worth to Bob Mitchell in Wynnewood, Indian Territory. (Courtesy Butch Moxley and Lynn Moxley)

RICHMOND, VIRGINIA, ca. 1870s. What's wrong with this picture?

TENNESSEE, ca. 1898. Well, maybe this little one didn't know he was breaking the rules when this picture was made, but a happy expression of this magnitude does deserve honorable mention.

In 1886, an English-born author, writing in America, introduced a book about a little boy who goes to live with his grandfather in England, where he becomes heir to a title and a fortune. The author was Frances Hodgson Burnett, and the book was *Little Lord Fauntleroy*. An immediate success, the novel featured a young boy whose hair was long and styled in ringlets, and whose clothes were elegant and frilly, accentuated by bows and lace.

The mothers of America, captivated by Little Lord Fauntleroy's perfection of wardrobe, as well as manners, set about transforming their own little boys into various versions of the novel's juvenile hero. For years, little boys would bear a resemblance to the fictional child in Frances Burnett's entertaining story, as illustrated in the following photographs of five southern boys.

BIRMINGHAM, ALABAMA, ca. 1905.

SAN ANTONIO, TEXAS, ca. 1889.

COLUMBIA, SOUTH CAROLINA, ca. 1900. "Harold Ernest Norwood at 6 years and 4 months." Made in Columbia Studio, at 1438¹/₂ Main Street.

TENNESSEE, ca. 1895.

DALLAS, TEXAS, ca. 1900.

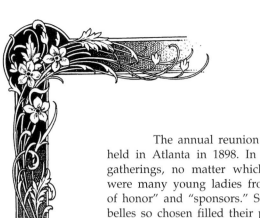

The annual reunion of the United Confederate Veterans was held in Atlanta in 1898. In keeping with the custom of these large gatherings, no matter which southern city hosted the event, there were many young ladies from all over Dixie who served as "maids of honor" and "sponsors." Such roles were quite prestigious, and the belles so chosen filled their positions with typical southern grace and charm. The UDC was ever present at the reunions, providing the girls with chaperones and instruction in etiquette. Thus was passed from generation to generation the elements of charm, protocol, and pageantry which once belonged wholly to the southern woman.

The *Confederate Veteran*'s August issue of 1898, in reporting the Atlanta reunion, contained photographs — ten of which are reproduced here — of several of the young ladies who served at that convention.

Miss Jennie Van Hoose, First Maid of Honor, Alabama Division.

Miss Anna B. Johnson, Maid of Honor, Kentucky Division.

Miss Mary S. Semple, Sponsor for Kentucky.

Miss Marguerite Sloan, Maid of Honor, South Carolina Division.

Miss Lillian Roden, Sponsor for Alabama.

Miss Florence Blair, Sponsor for Texas.

Miss Mimi Polk Horner, Maid of Honor, Arkansas.

Miss Ora Selma Maxey, Maid of Honor, Oklahoma Territory.

Miss Louise Harrison Beall, First Maid of Honor, Maryland.

Miss Emmie Sweet James, Sponsor for South Carolina.

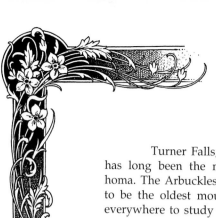

Turner Falls, located in the heart of the Arbuckle Mountains, has long been the most popular recreation area of southern Oklahoma. The Arbuckles, located about six miles south of Davis, are said to be the oldest mountains in the world, and geologists come from everywhere to study their unusual rock formations and the travertine deposits of Honey Creek, the spring-fed stream which forms the 77-foot falls.

These pictures illustrate the popularity of the falls nearly one hundred years ago. All five of the photographs used here are thought to have been made in 1895 or 1896. (Courtesy Butch Moxley and Lynn Moxley)

The seven couples enjoying this warm summer day at the falls are from Wynnewood. Several of them can be identified. The first man on the left is either Ed Strange or Frank Cochran. The next young man sitting and looking this way is Bob Mitchell. Sitting next to him is Delia Wilkerson. The man in the center of the picture, seated and holding a stick, is T.S. Shirley. Standing just above him is Sam Secrest, and the lady dressed in white, wearing a black hat, is thought to be Sam's wife. The gentleman in the foreground, resting on his elbow, is Garland Strange, and the two people at upper right are Sallie Lawrence and Joe Garrett.

(Opposite page) An unidentified group of people enjoying a picnic in the rugged Arbuckle Mountains. In the bottom photograph, they are exploring the caves and enjoying the water at Turner Falls. Several of them are carrying a newfangled camera called a Kodak, introduced by Eastman in 1888.

A group of young people — with chaperones, as was the custom of the day — ready to open up their picnic baskets on a rocky slope in the Arbuckle Mountains. All of these people are probably from Wynnewood, although only three can be identified. Penn Rabb is the third person from the left on the second row. Minnie Cooper, in the center, wears a white blouse with dark collar and belt and a pair of gloves. Directly behind her is Rushie Lael, granddaughter of Cyrus Harris, governor of the Chickasaw Nation during the War. On the back of this photograph, the photographer — also from Wynnewood — stamped his identification: *Photo by T.S. SHIRLEY, An Amateur.*

Photographs made during the War for Southern Independence cannot help but evoke bittersweet memories among southerners, for even the slightest realization of the horrors visited upon the South during those years arouses a sense of sadness and sympathy. Especially is this the case with pictures of lovely southern women who appear both composed and resilient, yet somehow a bit melancholy. Left behind to guard hearth and home, they were ill-equipped to defend against the blue horde which swept Dixie like a prairie fire in winter. Virtually unarmed, for southern men had to bear their own arms at the outset of the War, the women of the South were at the mercy of every soldier, straggler, and scavenger attendant to the Army of the United States.

While able-bodied men were defending the borders of the South, the interior lay unguarded. When Federal armies penetrated the heartland, they found no opposition save women, girls, small boys, and old men. The old men were often hung or imprisoned, leaving women and children to endure whatever degradation came their way.

Hunter, Sheridan, Butler, and Sherman were among the worst offenders. General Sherman made no pretense at civility, crassly proclaiming his intentions of making war upon the women and children of the South, a concept he vainly referred to as "total war." He bragged that he would "make Georgia howl" and would make war "so terrible that when peace comes it will last. . . . There is a class of people at the South who must be exterminated before there can be peace in the land." Upon commencing his infamous march to the sea, he warned the helpless inhabitants of Georgia that if they "burn forage and corn on our route, houses, barns and cotton gins must also be burned to keep them company."

Sherman needed no excuses. He was ready to burn. William Gilmore Simms, poet, author, and eyewitness to the burning of Columbia, South Carolina, said that Sherman's "hellhounds" were "well

A lady of Richmond.

prepared with all the appliances essential to their work. They did not need the torch. They carried with them, from house to house, pots and vessels containing combustible liquids, composed probably of phosphorous and other similar agents, turpentine, etc., and with balls of cotton saturated in this liquid, with which they also overspread the floors and walls, they conveyed the flames with wonderful rapidity from dwelling to dwelling. Each had his ready box of Lucifer matches, and, with a scrape upon the walls, the flames began to rage."

After the burning of Columbia, the braggard turned liar. In a vain attempt to demoralize South Carolinians, Sherman spread rumors that their own fellow-Columbian, General Wade Hampton, had fired the city during the retreat; however, when called to testify in some cotton cases after the War, Sherman admitted his guilt.

Mary Ames of South Carolina.

QUESTION: Were you at any time before crossing the Savannah River, or before reaching Columbia, aware of a spirit of vengeance — a desire of vengeance — animating your troops to be wreaked upon South Carolina?

ANSWER: I was; the felling was universal; and pervaded all ranks.

QUESTION: Officers and all?

ANSWER: Officers and all; we looked upon South Carolina as the cause of our woes.

QUESTION: And thought she thoroughly deserved strong treatment?

ANSWER: Yes, sir; that she thoroughly deserved extirpation.

Major George Ward Nichols, of Sherman's command, accosted a southern lady who had said that the South would never submit to subjugation by the north. "If you are defeated you will; and then you will have thoroughly learned what your people have never, before the war, in the slightest degree understood — *how to respect us.*"

His diary, kept on the march to the sea, reveals the arrogance with which the Yankees intimidated, insulted, and terrorized the women of Georgia and South Carolina.

The solemn truth is, that the Southern people have never had any conception of the National Idea. They do not know what it is to be an American. . . . The higher classes represent the scum, and the lower the dregs of civilization. They are South Carolinians, not Americans. . . . Our work has been the next thing to annihilation. . . . The extensive depot at Millen [Georgia] was a wooden structure of exceedingly graceful proportions. It was ignited in three places simultaneously, and its destruction was a brilliant spectacle; the building burning slowly, although there was sufficient wind to lift the vast volume of smoke and exhibit the exquisite architecture traced in lines of fire. This scene was so striking that even the rank and file observed and made comments upon it . . . for the taste for conflagrations has been so cultivated of late in the army that any small affair of that kind attracts very little attention. . . . Nearly all these places are deserted, although here and there we find children, whom it is difficult to persuade that they are not at once to be murdered. . . .

It may be for the good of future generations that this Rebel horde should be swept from the earth. . . . The 20th Corps . . . [met] a force . . . composed of a portion of . . . cavalry, militia, and a band of convicts who had been liberated from the penitentiary upon the condition that they would join the army. The most of these desperadoes have been taken prisoners, dressed in their state prison clothing. General Sherman has turned them loose, believing that Governor Brown has not got the full benefits of his liberality. . . .

As rumors of the approach of our army reached the frightened inhabitants, frantic efforts were made to conceal not only their valuable personal effects, plate, jewelry, and other rich goods, but also articles of food. . . . The favorite method of concealment was the burial of the treasures in the pathways and gardens adjoining the dwelling-houses. Sometimes, also, the graveyards were selected as the best place of security. . . . Wherever the army halted, almost every inch of ground . . . was poked by ramrods, pierced with sabres, or upturned with spades. . . . It was comical to see a group of these red-bearded, barefooted, ragged veterans punching the unoffending earth. . . . If they "struck a vein" a spade was instantly put in requisition, and the coveted wealth was speedily unearthed. Nothing escaped the observation of these sharp-witted soldiers. A woman standing upon the porch of a house . . . instantly became an object of suspicion, and she was watched until some movement betrayed a place of concealment. . . . It was all fair spoil of war, and the search made one of the excitements of the march.

U.S. Soldiers, in uniform, committed outrages of every description. Stealing jewelry directly off the person of a woman must have given them a perverted sense of command. They ripped earrings out of the ears of women, young and old alike, and breast pins were savagely torn from blouses and dresses. Lt. Thomas J. Myers, of Massachusetts, wrote his wife, bragging of the fine cache of jewelry so obtained.

We have had a glorious time in this State. Unrestricted license to plunder and burn was the order of the day. . . . Gold

Susan Bradford of Leon County, Florida.

watches, silver pitchers, cups, spoons, forks . . . are as common in camp as blackberries. . . . Officers over the rank of captain are not made to put their plunder in the estimate for general distribution. This is very unfair . . . and privates keep everything back that they can carry . . . such as rings, ear-rings, breast pins, etc., etc., of which, if I live to get home, I have a quart . . . and some No. 1 diamond rings and pins among them. General Sherman has enough gold to start a bank. His share in gold watches and chains alone at Columbia was 275. . . . Tell Lottie I am saving a pearl bracelet and earrings for her. . . . They were taken from the Misses Jamison.

These photographs, generally dating back to the War years (1861-1865), are interspersed with diary excerpts and letters of southern women who endured the ordeal. Looking at the photographs — some identified, some not — it is hard to imagine these women and children as targets of an American army; but the narrative, vivid and disturbing, reveals the terror experienced by most of the helpless inhabitants of the South, leaving little doubt as to the debauchery and barbarism of those wandering men in blue.

Children of Richmond, Virginia.

LEXINGTON, VIRGINIA, *June 1864* — From the diary of Cornelia Peake McDonald.

Our house was struck in several places but no harm done. Indeed, I was passed being frightened by shot and shell. . . . We had been engaged all the morning in hiding the things we thought might be taken from us, among the rest a few hens and chickens that I had been trying to raise. The children quickly caught them and transported them to a garret where we also put a few other things that might tempt them, the silver, etc. I was passing by the stairs and saw Hunter sitting on the lowest step crying bitterly. I stopped to kiss and comfort my poor little three year old baby and asked him what the matter was, when amid his sobs, he said, "The Yankees are coming to our house and they will take all our breakfast and will capture me and Fanny.". . . We remained as quiet as possible all the afternoon while the town was alive with soldiers plundering and robbing the inhabitants. Some came into our yard, robbed the milk house of its contents . . . picking up everything they could use or destroy. . . .

At sunset we saw a man led by with a file of soldiers. The children came in and told me that it was Capt. Matt White, that they were taking him out to shoot him. I thought they knew nothing about it and gave the matter no attention.

Sunday began a fearful work. The Virginia Military Institute with all the professors' houses was set on fire, and the distracted families amid the flames were rushing about trying to save some of their things, when they were forced to leave them, officers standing by for the purpose. . . . Negroes were seen scudding away in all directions bearing away the spoils of the burning barracks — books, furniture, trunks full of the clothes of the absent cadets. . . .

On looking down the street in the direction of Gov. Letcher's house I saw it on fire. I instantly put on my bonnet and ran down there to help Mrs. Letcher . . . and so in breathless haste got there in time to see the house enveloped in flames. Mrs. Letcher had consented to entertain two officers at her house, that she had been civilly asked to do. They had spent the night, and eaten breakfast with the family, sociably chatting all the while.

When they rose from breakfast, one of them, Capt. Berry, informed Mrs. Letcher that he should immediately set fire to her home. He took a bottle of benzine . . . and pouring it on the sofas and curtains in the lower rooms, applied a match, and then proceeded up stairs. Mrs. Letcher ran up stairs and snatching her sleeping baby from the cradle, rushed from the house with it, leaving everything she had to the flames. Lizzy ran up stairs and went into her father's room to secure some of his clothes, and had hung over her arm some of his linen, when Capt. Berry came near her with a lighted match, and set fire to the clothes as they hung on her arm. He then gathered all the family clothing and bedding into a pile in the middle of the room and set fire to them.

When I reached the scene, Mrs. Letcher was sitting on a stone in the street with her baby on her lap sleeping and her other little children gathered around. She sat tearless and calm, but it was a pitiable group, sitting there with their burning house for a background to the picture.

Some officers who had stayed all night at Mr. Matthew White's, and breakfasted there, had in reply to the anxious inquiries of the poor old Mother about her son . . . assured her that he was in the jail just opposite her house; that he was temporarily detained, but would be immediately released. That afternoon as I sat by the window I saw a wagon pass on its way up the street, and in it a stiff, straight form covered with a sheet. It was poor Matt White on his way to his Mother. He had been taken out to the woods and shot as the children had said, and had been left where he fell. Mrs. Cameron's daughters hearing the firing, went down to the place when the party had left, and finding the poor body, stayed there by it all night to keep it from being mangled by animals. No men were near to do it, and they kept up their watch . . . till the troops had left.

The next day, Wednesday, was his funeral. Everybody who knew the family was there, I among the rest. We went to the cemetery and saw the poor fellow buried.

MARSHALL COUNTY, MISSISSIPPI, *January 27, 1863* — From a letter by Cordelia Lewis Scales to her friend, Lou Irby.

. . . Thirty or forty of the Yankees would rush in at a time, take everything to eat they could lay their hands on, & break, destroy & steal everything they wanted to. . . . I'll tell you what I thought we would certainly starve. One thousand black republicans, the 26th Illinois, camped in our groves, for two weeks. . . . The next set that camped on us was the 90th Illinois Irish Legion. . . .

The next we had were the "Grierson Thieves" & the next the 7th Kansas Jay Hawkers. I can't write of these; it makes my blood boil to think of the outrages they committed. They tore the ear rings out of the ladies' ears, pulled their rings & breast pins off, took them by the hair; threw them down & knocked them about. One of them sent me word that they shot ladies as well as men, & if I did not stop talking to them so & displaying my Confederate flag, he'd blow my brains out. I sent him word by the lady that I did not expect anything better from Yankees, but he must remember two could play at that game. . . .

Lou, I tell you what we've been through fiery trials, and if we did not exactly cuss, there is a great many of us *that thought* cuss mighty strong.

JEFFERSON COUNTY, VIRGINIA, *July 20, 1864* — A letter from Henrietta Bedinger to U.S. General David Hunter.

Yesterday your underling, Captain Martindale, of the First New York Cavalry, executed your infamous order and burned my house. . . . I, therefore, a helpless woman whom you have cruelly wronged, address you, a Major-General of the United States army, and demand why this was done? What was my offence? My husband was absent, an exile. He had never been a politician or in any way engaged in the struggle now going on, his age preventing. This fact your chief of staff, David Strother, could have told you. The house was built by my father, a Revolutionary soldier, who served the whole seven years for your independence. There was I born; there the sacred dead repose. It was my house and my home, and there has your niece (Miss Griffith), who has tarried among us all this horrid war up to the present time, met

Issa D. Breckinridge of Lexington, Kentucky.

with all kindness and hospitality at my hands. Was it for this that you turned me, my young daughter, and little son out upon the world without a shelter? Or was it because my husband is the grandson of the Revolutionary patriot and "rebel," Richard Henry Lee, and the near kinsman of the noblest of Christian warriors, the greatest of generals, Robert E. Lee? Heaven's blessing be upon his head forever. You and your Government have failed to conquer, subdue, or match him; and disappointment, rage, and malice find vent on the helpless and inoffensive.

Hyena-like, you have torn my heart to pieces! for all hallowed memories clustered around that homestead, and demon-like you have done it without even the pretext of revenge, for I never saw or harmed you. Your office is not to lead, like a brave man and soldier, your men to fight in the ranks of war, but your work has been to separate yourself from all danger, and with your incendiary band steal unaware upon helpless women and children, to insult and destroy. Two fair homes did you yesterday ruthlessly lay in ashes, giving not a moment's warning to the startled inmates of your wicked purpose; turning mothers and children out of doors, you are execrated by your own men for the cruel work you give them to do.

In the case of Colonel A.R. Boteler, both father and mother were far away. Any heart but that of Captain Martindale (and yours) would have been touched by that little circle, comprising a widowed daughter just risen from her bed of illness, her fatherless babies — the oldest not five years old — and her heroic sister. I repeat, any man would have been touched at that sight but Captain Martindale. One might as well hope to find mercy and feeling in the heart of a wolf bent on his prey of young lambs, as to search for such qualities in his bosom. You have chosen well your agent for such deeds, and doubtless will promote him. . . .

I ask who that does not wish infamy and disgrace attached to him forever would serve under you? Your name will stand on history's page as the Hunter of weak women, and innocent children, the Hunter to destroy defenceless villages and refined and beautiful homes — to torture afresh the agonized hearts of widows; the Hunter of Africa's poor sons and daughters, to lure them on to ruin and death of soul and body; the Hunter with the relentless heart of a wild beast, the face of a fiend and the form of a man. Oh, Earth, behold the monster! Can I say "God forgive you?" No prayer can be offered for you. Were it possible for human lips to raise your name heavenward, angels would thrust the foul thing back again, and demons claim their own. The curses of thousands, the scorns of manly and upright, and the hatred of the true and honorable, will follow you and yours through all time, and brand your name infamy! infamy!

Again, I demand why you have burned my home? Answer as you must answer before the Searcher of all hearts, why have you added this cruel, wicked deed to your many crimes?

LIBERTY COUNTY, GEORGIA, *December 17, 1864* — From the journal of Mary Jones.

About four o'clock this morning we were roused by the sound of horses; and Sue, our faithful woman, came upstairs breathless with dismay and told us they had come upon the most dreadful intent, and had sent her in to tell me what it was, and had inquired if there were any young women in my family. Oh, the agony — the agony of that awful hour no language can describe! No heart can conceive it. . . . We all knelt down around the bed and went to prayer; and we continued in silent prayer a long time. Kate prayed, Daughter prayed, and I prayed; and the dear little children . . . knelt down beside us. And there we were, alone and unprotected, imploring protection from a fate worse than death. . . . We looked out of the window and saw one man pacing before the courtyard gate . . . and we afterwards found he had voluntarily undertaken to guard the house. In this we felt that our prayers had been signally answered.

*December 24* — As we were finishing our breakfast . . . five Yankees made their appearance. . . . One knocked at the door. . . . "I have come to search your house . . . and I mean to do it. . . . This house will make a beautiful fire and a great smoke.". . .

Again they surveyed the house, asked if I knew North and South Hampton, said they had just burnt both places, that my house would be a beautiful flame, and that night they would return and burn it down. . . .

We have all spent a miserable day. . . . The darkness of night is around our dwelling. We are all upstairs in one room with closed windows and a dim light. Our poor little children have eaten their supper . . . and they have been put to bed with their clothes on, that they may be ready to move at an instant's notice. . . .

*January 4* — Dr. Harris . . . came without delay and in the face of danger. . . . Soon after being in her room he requested a private interview, informing me that my child was in a most critical condition, and I must be prepared for the worst. . . . During these hours of agony the yard was filled with Yankees. . . . They were all around the

A lady of Arkansas.

house; my poor child . . . amid her agony of body, could hear their . . . wild halloos and cursing beneath her windows. Our dear friend Kate King had to meet them alone. She entreated that they would not come in or make a noise, for there was sickness in the house. They replied: "We are not as bad as you think us. We will take off our spurs and come in." And one actually pushed by her and came in.

She stepped upon the porch and implored if there was one spark of humanity or honor about them that they would not come in, saying: "You compel me to speak plainly. There is a child being born this very instant in this house, and if there is an officer or a gentleman amongst you I entreat you to protect the house from intrusion." After a while they left, screaming and yelling in a most fiendish way as they rode from the house.

*January 7* — As I stand and look at the desolating changes wrought by the hand of an inhuman foe . . . I can enter into the feelings of Job. . . . All our pleasant things are laid low. . . . We are prisoners in our own home; we dare not open windows or doors. Sometimes our little children are allowed under a strict watch and guard to run a little in the sunshine, but it is always under constant apprehension. The poor little creatures at a moment's warning — just let them hear "Yankee coming!" — rush in and remain almost breathless, huddled together in one of the upper rooms like a bevy of frightened partridges. To obtain a mouthful of food we have been obliged to cook in what was formerly our drawing room; and I have to rise every morning by candle-light, before the dawn of day, that we may have it before the enemy arrives to take it from us. And then sometimes we and the dear little ones have not chance to eat again before dark. . . . Do the annals of civilized — and may I add savage — warfare afford any record of brutality equaled in extent and duration to that which we have suffered, and which has been inflicted on us by the Yankees? . . . Officers and men have alike engaged in this work of degradation. I scarcely know how we have stood up under it. God alone has enabled us to "speak with the enemy in the gates," and calmly, without a tear, to see my house broken open, entered with false keys, threatened to be burned to ashes, refused food and ordered to be starved to death, told that I had no right even to wood or water, that I should be "humbled in the very dust I walked upon," a pistol and carbine presented to my breast, cursed and reviled as a rebel, a hypocrite, a devil. Every servant, on pain of having their brains blown out, is forbidden to wait upon us or furnish us food. Every trunk, bureau, box, room, closet has been opened or broken open and searched, and whatever was wanted . . . taken.

*January 17* — Sometimes, when our hearts have fainted and our strength failed as we were surrounded by our foes, we have knelt and prayed together, and God has given us strength. . . . I never knew before the power or calming influence of prayer. . . . We must have died but for prayer.


LIBERTY COUNTY, GEORGIA, *December 16, 1864* — From the journal of Mary S. Mallard.

By the time Mother and I could get downstairs we saw forty or fifty men in the pantry, flying hither and thither, ripping open the safe with their swords and breaking open the crockery cupboards. . . . Mother had some chickens and ducks roasted and put in the safe for our family. These the men seized whole, tearing them to pieces with their teeth like ravenous beasts. They were clamorous for whiskey. . . .

They flew around the house, tearing open boxes and everything that was closed. They broke open Mother's little worktable with an andiron . . . Failing to find treasure, they took the sweet little locks of golden hair that her mother had cut from the heads of her angel children near a half century ago, and scattering them upon the floor trampled them under their feet. . . . A number of them went into the attic . . . and carried off twelve bushels of meal Mother had stored. . . . She told them they were taking all she had to support herself and daughter, a friend, and five little children. Scarcely one regarded even the sound of her voice; those who did laughed and . . . only left some rice which they did not want, and poured out a quart or so of meal upon the floor. At other times they said they meant to starve us to death.

It is impossible to imagine the . . . yelling, cursing, quarreling, and running from one room to another in wild confusion. . . . Their throats were open sepulchres, their mouths filled with cursing and bitterness and lies. These men belonged to Kilpatrick's cavalry.

*December 19* — Squads of Yankees came all day. . . . The women, finding it entirely unsafe for them to be out of the house at all, would run in and conceal themselves. . . . The few remaining chickens and some sheep were killed. These men were so outrageous at the Negro houses that the Negro men were obliged to stay at their houses for the protection of their wives; and in some instances they rescued them from the hands of these infamous creatures.

*December 20* — A squad of Yankees came soon after breakfast. Needing a chain . . . they went to the well and took it from the well bucket. Mother went out and entreated them not to take it from the well, as it was our means of getting water. They replied: "You have no right to have even wood or water," and immediately took it away.

A little boy from Russellville, Kentucky.

*December 21* — Six of Kilpatrick's cavalry rode up. . . . They . . . thundered at the door. . . . Mother opened it, when one of them presented a pistol to her breast and demanded why she dared to keep her house closed. . . . She told them her house had been four times searched in every part, and everything taken from it. . . . With horrible oaths they rode off, shooting two ducks in the yard. . . . Later in the afternoon more came and carried off the few remaining ducks. Going to the Negro houses, they called Cato, the driver, and told him they knew he was feeding "that _____ old heifer in the house," and they would "blow his _____ brains out if he gave her another morsel to eat, for they meant to starve her to death. . . .

*December 27* — No enemy today. Bless the Lord for this mercy!

*December 28* — Another day without the appearance of the Yankees. Could we but know we should be spared one day we would breathe freely, but we are in constant apprehension and terror. . . . Was there ever any civilized land given up for such a length of time to lawless pillage and brutal inhumanities?

*December 29* — Three Yankees and one Negro came up. . . . Three came to the door, and after knocking violently several times one broke open the door. . . . They insisted upon coming in, and asked for that "_____ wench" that had locked the door, threatening to "shoot her _____ brains out," using the Saviour's name in awful blasphemy. . . . One went into the parlor and pantry and into one or two other rooms; and one went into the room we are compelled to cook in, and crouched like a beast over the fire. He was black and filthy as a chimney sweep. Indeed, such is the horrible odor they leave in the house we can scarcely endure it.

COLUMBIA, SOUTH CAROLINA, *December 31, 1864* — From the diary of Emma LeConte.

Sherman the brute avows his intention of converting South Carolina into a wilderness. Not one house, he says, shall be left standing, and his licentious troops — whites and negroes — shall be turned loose to ravage and violate. . . .

*February 15* — They tell me the streets in town are lined with panic-stricken crowds, trying to escape. All is confusion and turmoil. . . .

*February 17* — Well, they are here. . . . I ran upstairs to my bedroom windows just in time to see the U.S. flag run up over the State House. Oh, what a horrid sight! What a degradation! After four long bitter years of bloodshed and hatred, now to float there at last! That hateful symbol of despotism! . . .

A little girl of Richmond.

*February 18* — What a night of horror, misery, and agony! . . . We could hear their shouts as they surged down Main Street. . . . Night drew on. . . . Before me the whole southern horizon was lit by camp fires which dotted the woods. On one side the sky was illuminated by the burning of Gen. Hampton's residence. . . . By the red glare we could watch the wretches walking — generally staggering — back and forth from the camp to town — shouting — hurrahing — cursing South Carolina — swearing — blaspheming — singing ribald songs and using such obscene language that we were forced to go indoors. . . . The drunken devils roamed about, setting fire to every house. . . . They were fully equipped for the noble work they had in hand. Each soldier was furnished with combustibles compactly put up. They would enter houses in the presence of helpless women and children, pour turpentine on the beds and set them on fire. . . .

The wretched people rushing from their burning homes were not allowed to keep even the few necessaries they gathered up in their flight — even blankets and food were taken from them. . . . The College buildings caught. . . . All the physicians and nurses were on the roof trying to save the buildings, and the poor wounded inmates, left to themselves, such as could crawled out while those who could not move waited to be burned to death.

The Common opposite the gate was crowded with homeless women and children . . . shivering in the night air. Such a scene as this with the drunken, fiendish soldiery in their dark uniforms, infuriated, cursing, screaming, exulting in their work, came nearer realizing the material ideal of hell than anything I ever expect to see again. They call themselves "Sherman's Hellhounds." . . .

We do not know the extent of the destruction, but we are told that the greater portion of the town is in ashes — perhaps the loveliest town in all our Southern country. This is civilized warfare. This is the way in which the "cultured" Yankee nation wars upon women and children! Failing with our men in the field, *this* is the way they must conquer! I suppose there was scarcely an able bodied man, except the hospital physicians, in the whole twenty thousand people. It is so easy to burn the homes over the heads of helpless women and children, and turn them with insults and sneers into the streets. One expects these people to lie and steal, but it does seem such an outrage even upon degraded humanity that those who practise such wanton and useless cruelty should call themselves men. It seems to us even a contamination to look at these devils. Think of the degradation of being conquered and ruled by such a people! It seems to me now as if we would choose extermination. . . .

From what I hear, their chief aim, while taunting helpless women, has been to "humble their pride" — "Southern pride." "Where now," they would say, "is all your pride — see what we have brought you to! This is what you get for setting yourselves up as better than other folks." The women acted with quiet dignity and refused to lower themselves by any retort. Someone told me the following: Some soldiers were pillaging the house of a lady. One asked her if they had not humbled her pride *now*. "No, indeed," she said, "nor can you ever." "You *fear* us anyway." "No," she said. "By ____, but you *shall* fear me," and he cocked his pistol and put it to her head. "Are you afraid now?" She folded her arms and, looking him steadily in the eye, said contemptuously, "No." He dropped his pistol, and with an exclamation of admiration, left her.

*February 19* — Their horrid old gridiron of a flag is flaunting its bars in our faces all day. Ever since dark thick clouds of smoke have been rolling up. . . . *How I hate* the people who have done this! . . .

*February 21* — I wonder if the vengeance of heaven will not pursue such fiends! Before they came here, I thought I hated them as much as was possible — now I know there are no limits to the feeling of hatred. . . .

*February 22* — It was dreadful — everything was burst open — all our silver and valuables stolen — articles of clothing slashed up by bayonets and burned. . . .

*February 23* — The Yankees talk very strongly of conquering the South. . . . I would rather endure any poverty than live under Yankee rule. I would rather far have France or any other country for a mistress — anything but live as one nation with *Yankees* — that word in my mind is a synonym for *all* that is *mean,* despicable and abhorrent. . .

*March 1* — There was a rumor afloat yesterday that a *negro* regiment was marching from Branchville to garrison Columbia. Heavens! Have we not suffered enough? I do not believe it, but the very thought is enough to make one shudder. . . .

*March 10* — Uncle John . . . had a hard time with

A lady of Missouri.

the Yankees. . . . The officer looked surprised and shocked. "Why cannot you yield?" he asked. Uncle John shrugged his shoulders and said we would resort to anything rather than give up. "Well," replied the Yankee, "I hope the South won't do anything of that kind, for of course in that event we would not spare or respect your women.". . .

*May 18* — We were visited yesterday by a squad of Yankees, . . the first that have been in Columbia since the 20th of February. . . . The negroes throng around them and they affiliate pleasantly with their colored brethren — even affectionately. They lie beside them on the grass and walk the streets with the negro girls, calling them "young ladies" — and why not? Doubtless they recognize in them not only their equals, but their superiors. *Perhaps* negroes *may* come in contact with them without being degraded, but I doubt it, for the negro is an imitative race. He has been elevated to some extent but will quickly retrograde in associating with such white people as these. Dear me! How the sight of that blue uniform makes my blood boil! . . .

*May 28* — These Yankee officers . . . take it rather hard that they are treated so coldly. . . . Horton especially seems to feel it that he is cut off so absolutely from the society of ladies. Great Heavens! What do they expect? They invade our country, murder our people, desolate our homes, conquer us, subject us to every indignity and humiliation — and then we must offer our hands with pleasant smiles and invite them to our houses, entertain them perhaps with "Southern hospitality" — all because sometimes they act with common decency and humanity! Are they crazy? What do they think we are made of?

Sallie Cummins of Hickman County, Tennessee.

Rhoda Thornton Cartledge of Barbour County, Alabama.

A lady of Richmond.

When the guns fell silent, an uneasy calm settled in and over the devastated South, but only for a moment — or what seemed like only a moment. No sooner had the eerie silence of blackened chimneys and freshly dug graves contrasted themselves with the gaiety and jollity of the pre-War South than it happened that southerners witnessed the jamming of virtually every dusty road in their desolate country with a scourge hitherto unknown — the carpetbagger.

Lowest of the low, this northern predator descended upon the decimated South with one primary aim — enriching himself. Whatever he had to do, he was not above it. Helpless widows, orphaned children, soldiers maimed by war, the elderly, the poor, the benighted negro — all were fair game to this miscreant. With southern cities under federal military rule, white men disfranchised, and every male negro on the voting rolls (in multiple precincts), the carpetbagger saw at once the political opportunities available to his pursuit of wealth. And a new reign of terror began.

The Freedmen's Bureau of the U.S. Government was a front for political subversion, and the newly arrived carpetbagger found welcome advantage in the machinery of the enterprise. The life of the negro began to revolve around the Bureau, and it was easy to convince the now-unemployed and impressionable colored population, who had flocked to shanty towns around the edges of southern cities, that all of their many problems were the direct result of the southern white man. The idle negroes were convened in meetings, day after day, week after week, month after month, and told how evil were the white people of the South. As the rhetoric became more inflammatory, meeting sites shifted from negro schoolhouses to secret places in the woods. Here, carpetbaggers urged them to acts of violence and intimidation against native southerners — acts which were all too often carried out to the letter.

Gangs of roving negroes fired weapons into houses along residential streets and pushed ladies — and gentlemen — off the sidewalks, often spitting on them and yelling insults. Their foul mouths cursed men and women alike. Encouraged by their carpetbag mentors, blacks escalated the attacks until barns were being burned in the dead of night, houses were being torched in rapid succession, and widowed women were not safe from personal attack at any hour of the day. All the while, the carpetbag "friends" of the illiterate and uneducated negro were selling him little blue back spellers, available at the meetings, with the admonition that the words contained in the

322

little book would make him an instant Solomon. Bought for less than 10 cents on the dollar, the books were sold to the unknowing negro for the exorbitant price of one dollar apiece.

The world knows the story of the Ku Klux Klan. Riding in the dark of night, southern men reclaimed the South from the black terror. Carpetbag rule was overthrown; civil law was reinstituted; and, negro rampage was summarily ended. Most of the disorder was over by 1869, but it is thought that some Klan orders were still in operation as late as 1877, when in that year the last Federal troops were pulled out of Dixie.

Photographs of Ku Klux Klan robes are quite rare, due mainly to the secretive nature of the organization. The robes shown here are homemade, of course, and date back to the late 1860s and early '70s. They are especially interesting in that they exemplify the diversity of style in early Klan robes. Many of the earlier robes were black, red, purple, and various shades of other dark colors, rather than the white to which we are generally accustomed. Stars, half-moons, circles, crosses, and diamonds of bright-colored cloth

embellished the uniforms to give them a bizarre, supernatural look intended to frighten the superstitious negroes into mending their ways. To the carpetbagger, the hood represented the most frightening aspect, for it disguised the identity of the Klansman, effectively denying a victim any kind of retaliation.

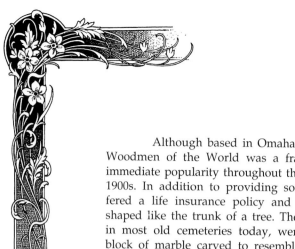

Although based in Omaha, Nebraska, where it was founded, Woodmen of the World was a fraternal organization which gained immediate popularity throughout the South during the 1890s and early 1900s. In addition to providing social activities, the organization offered a life insurance policy and an impressive marble tombstone, shaped like the trunk of a tree. The monuments, which can be found in most old cemeteries today, were tall and usually rested upon a block of marble carved to resemble a stack of freshly cut logs.

Woodmen of the World chapters, composed of men, were called "camps." Women could also buy the life insurance policy, and those who did were eligible for membership in women's chapters called "groves." Today, the organization is much larger than it was, but increasing numbers have culminated in structural changes. Now, men and women are usually enrolled in the same chapter, and the old terminology has given way to the new, so that camps and groves are replaced with the term "lodge."

Tombstones are no longer provided, due to the expense involved, but small grave markers are available to the policyholder. One thing that has not changed is the geographical strength of Woodmen of the World, that still being in the South. North Carolina leads the country with more lodges and members than any other state.

PAUL D. JACKSON.
BORN
Aug 11, 1863
DIED
Nov. 25, 1901
ERECTED BY THE
WOODMEN OF
THE WORLD

TELEPHONE, TEXAS, ca. 1901. The Telephone camp included many young men, only one of whom is positively identifiable in this picture — 26-year-old Andrew Jackson Burkes. He is the fourth man from the right on the back row. The second man from the right may be his brother, William Hilliard Burkes. Of the men who are kneeling, the fifth man from the left may be their half brother, Oscar Thompson. In 1916, Andrew Burkes passed away at the Mayo Clinic in Rochester, Minnesota, having gone there for treatment of stomach cancer by famed stomach surgeon, William James Mayo. Andrew was brought back to Wetumka, Oklahoma, and buried in the city cemetery. His wife, Eulalie, picked out the following verse for his Woodmen of the World monument.

> A loving one from us is gone,
> A voice we loved is stilled.
> A place is vacant in our home
> That never can be filled.

ARLINGTON, TEXAS, ca. 1900. (Opposite page) This photograph from the studio of A.J. McHaney was initially found interesting for its lighting contrast. Notice the artistic use of backlighting to create a light background against the man's dark suit while the lady's white blouse contrasts well with a dark background. Upon closer inspection, the gentleman's lapel pin turned out to be the insignia of Woodmen of the World.

WETUMKA, OKLAHOMA, ca. 1915. When Joseph Cullen Root founded the Woodmen of the World in 1890, one of his objectives was to see that no member of the Woodmen would ever rest in an unmarked grave. In addition to individual tombstones, the society erected memorial markers to noted Americans, such as the Bankheads in Alabama, Stephen Foster in Florida, and Zachary Taylor in Louisiana. In the case of military veterans, an unveiling was usually held at the gravesite. In this photograph, such a ceremony is taking place, the widow still dressed in her mourning clothes and standing beside her husband's monument in the cemetery. The only identifiable person in this dedication is Andrew Jackson Burkes, seventh man from the right.

SOMEWHERE IN THE SOUTH, PROBABLY TENNESSEE. ca. 1895. This photograph of the *W.K. Phillips* was found in Nashville and is thought to have been made on the Cumberland River or another of Tennessee's navigable rivers. It appears to have been chartered by the Woodmen of the World for an excursion. A large banner drapes the ballustrade of the second deck near the bow of this sternwheeler. (Courtesy Edwin P'Pool)

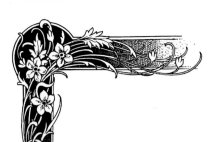

After the war, many southerners migrated westward. They were looking for a new start, trying to regenerate themselves in a new land. War and Reconstruction had taken a mighty toll, and as one old-timer explained, "all the good land was taken up here, so all we could do was look west." Some went to New Mexico, some to Arizona, and some all the way to California; but, most went only as far west as they could go and still be in the South. For the first twenty years after the War, that meant Texas. Land was still available in that vast state, and it was suitable to cotton production.

By the mid-1880s, railroads were pushing deep into the Indian Territory, where Indian land was being settled by white southerners under special agreements with the Five Civilized Tribes. By 1907, the eastern half of Oklahoma, populated nearly exclusively by Indians and settlers from the Old South, had 750,000 inhabitants. The great southern migration can be illustrated with the story of one emigrant named William Bethel Crump.

W.B. Crump was born in May, 1860, in Etowah County, Alabama, and it was in the public schools of that county that he received his education. His parents, Memory W. and Elizabeth P. Crump, were both natives of Georgia. In 1887, W.B. married Lucy Nuckolls, of Gadsden, Alabama, and in 1889 they left Alabama for the Indian Territory, arriving in the brand new town of Wynnewood. Crump's parents and small son made the trip with them. This photograph was made about 1908 at the Webb Studio in Ardmore, Oklahoma. (Courtesy Ben Crump)

Lucy Nuckolls was born January 6, 1862, in Hall County, Georgia, to James G. Lafayette Nuckolls and his wife, the former Elizabeth E. Moor, during the turmoil of the War. In January, 1864, her father enlisted as a private in Co. E, First Confederate Regiment, Georgia Volunteers. In December, he was killed at the Battle of Nashville, leaving a widow and three small daughters. The girls were sent to Gadsden, Alabama, to live with relatives, and it was in Gadsden that Lucy met and married W.B. Crump. This photograph was taken about 1880 in Rome, Georgia, when Lucy was about eighteen years old. (Courtesy Louise Neidermaier)

Lucy was in her early 30s when this picture was taken in Wynnewood in the early 1890s. Southerners brought their Old South traditions with them when they came to Indian Territory, and Lucy was an early member of the UDC chapter in Wynnewood, joining on the military record of her father. When she passed away February 23, 1933, after what the newspaper called "a long and severe illness," her obituary added, "Mrs. Crump, one of Wynnewood's pioneers, performed her part as a sterling citizen, interested in civic enterprise, devoted to her church, an exemplary mother, and a beloved friend. Her passing is mourned by all who knew her." (Courtesy Louise Niedermaier)

W.B. Crump's first business was a mercantile store. By 1895, he was entering the banking business, and in 1901 he built the Southern National Bank, pictured below in a photo taken about 1903. He was president of both the Southern National and First National Banks in Wynnewood. The postcard view above, taken about 1908, shows the home he built in 1896. W.B. Crump passed away in 1944 and is buried beside his wife, parents, and children in Wynnewood.

Three of the four children of W.B. and Lucy Crump are pictured here. The photograph of Bess was taken in 1906 or 1907. W.B., Jr. and Wilkie were photographed at Martin Brothers Studio in Wynnewood about 1905. At the time these pictures were taken, Earl, the oldest child and only one born in Alabama, was in Lebanon, Tennessee, where he attended Castle Heights Military School and Cumberland University.

Helen Keller was born June 27, 1880, in Tuscumbia, Alabama. Stricken by an illness at the age of 19 months, she was left blind and deaf. Unable to understand anyone and isolated from the world, she was a virtual prisoner in her own body. When Helen was seven years old, Anne Sullivan arrived from the Perkins Institution of Boston. One day at the pump, Anne ran water over one of Helen's hands while tapping out an alphabet code in the other. Suddenly, the door of Helen's mind opened, and by nightfall she had learned thirty words. Helen Keller became one of history's most remarkable women, writing and lecturing tirelessly for the betterment of others. Even before she died in 1968, her birthplace, *Ivy Green*, had become a permanent shrine, open to the admiring public. This photograph of Helen and Anne was probably made about 1901 in New York, where Helen had gone to work for the Institute of the Blind. (Courtesy *Ivy Green*)

DALLAS, TEXAS, 1925. (Opposite page) Silas C. Buck holds the flag of the 16th Confederate Cavlary, a unit made up partly in Mississippi and partly in Alabama. On April 12, 1865, he hid the flag from his captors at the Battle of Mobile. Years later, he wrote of the incident. "The colors were the last which ever floated over a Confederate line of battle east of the Mississippi. . . . I bore these colors in the fight, of which fact I feel proud. . . . Throwing away the staff, I hid the colors and thus saved them from surrender. Just before we separated I gave the colors to Col. Spence who has had them ever since. He brought them to Dallas and kindly allowed me to bring them home to show my family. Precious relics. I feel as if my child had come home after years of absence. . . . I was seventeen when we, not the colors, were surrendered, and I am inclined to believe I was one of the youngest, if not the youngest, color bearers in the Confederate army." This photograph was made at the UCV Reunion in Dallas. (Courtesy Kentucky Historical Society)

LADONIA, TEXAS, 1920. James Alexander Boyd, of Putnam County, Tennessee, is shown here in the UCV uniform he wore to the annual reunions of the United Confederate Veterans. Accompanied by his daughter, Zora Holleman, and with train tickets that entitled them to travel for a month, he seized the opportunity provided by the Houston reunion and spent the month visiting relatives in Texas. In this photo, he is surrounded by his son, Lem Boyd (standing); his daughter, Verna Osborne (standing next to Lem); her sons, Charles Wesley Osborne (standing in front of Lem), James Leslie Osborne (standing in front of Verna), and M.D. Osborne (standing in front of James); and the elderly veteran's other daughter, Edna Combs, who holds her daughter, Kathleen, on her lap. Boyd joined Co. K, 16th Tennessee Infantry, on June 9, 1861. Discharged due to ill health, he joined the cavalry on February 10, 1863, and served with Co. A, Allison's Cavalry, until captured and sent to a prison camp. After the War, he was a pillar of the community, living to the age of 83. A strict Methodist and Mason, his well-attended funeral was held on the front lawn of his home. (Courtesy James K. Turner)

MISSISSIPPI, ca. 1894. (Courtesy Elmore Greaves)

GEORGIA, ca. 1861. Like so many southern boys, Edwin Jennison left family and home and headed for the front when Yankee hordes swept southward. Never was so much required of one so young. Private Jennison was killed July 1, 1862, in Virginia at the Battle of Malvern Hill.

KENTUCKY, April 24, 1909. A reunion of Confederate veterans who proudly served with Gen. John Hunt Morgan, the swashbuckling cavalryman who dashed into Indiana and Ohio and did what all southerners wanted someone to do — spread terror into the smug, safe environs of the north! Posing for the camera are members of Company F, 2nd Kentucky Regiment, and their UDC sponsors.

MADISON COUNTY, MISSISSIPPI, ca. 1862. General Stephen Arne Decatur Greaves and two of his sons, Stephen Arne Decatur Greaves, Jr., and William Figures Greaves, at *Sunny Place Plantation* near Livingston. (Courtesy Elmore Greaves)

WILKINSON COUNTY, GEORGIA, April 24, 1866. It had been two years since William Green Lewis enlisted in the army, and it had been one year since the end of the War, but William was so proud of his Confederate uniform that he got married in it. That's the day this ambrotype was made. It mattered little to William that the uniform was too big. After all, he was only 15 when he joined Company D of the 8th Regiment of Georgia Militia. What mattered to William was his love for the Confederacy and that uniform, a feeling shared by his descendants today. (Courtesy Miriam Brown)

MISSISSIPPI, ca. 1913. (Opposite page) This is the kind of store that kept farmers in business. Here they could buy implements, feed, seed, overalls, and tools. (Courtesy Elmore Greaves)

SEWANEE, TENNESSEE, ca. 1900. (Opposite page) A Confederate Veterans Reunion in the yard at Miss Sally Milhado's house. The only people identified here are Uncle Bob, first man from the left, and Dr. DuBose, seated at the end of the table in the foreground. (Courtesy University of the South)

PEWEE VALLEY, KENTUCKY, 1904. Confederate veterans while away the hours in the comfortable sitting room of the Confederate Home, founded in 1902 to take care of Kentucky's aging soldiers. In a state bitterly divided by the War, the majority of its soldiers having sided with the Lincoln regime, it is ironic that the Home for Confederate Soldiers was established in the northern part of the state, only ten miles from the Indiana state line. (Courtesy Kentucky Historical Society)

ALABAMA, ca. 1862. Brig. General Sterling A.M. Wood, of Gen. Pat Cleburne's Division, CSA. Wood had served earlier under Gen. Albert Sidney Johnston, who was killed at Shiloh. After the War, Gen. Wood served in the Alabama state legislature during 1882 and 1883. He was a member of the law faculty of the University of Alabama during the 1889-90 term. Born in Florence on March 17, 1823, he died at Tuscaloosa on Jan. 26, 1891. (Courtesy Albert Baxendale, Jr.)

NASHVILLE, TENNESSEE, 1899. Miss Tennie Painter. (Courtesy Edwin P'Pool)

NASHVILLE, TENNESSEE, ca. 1908. The Confederate Soldiers Home, the central portion of which is shown here, was constructed in 1894 on land originally belonging to Andrew Jackson. The state had bought the remaining 500 acres of Jackson's estate in 1859. Thirty years later, when it proposed using the deteriorating mansion as a home for Confederate veterans, several local women swung into action to oppose the plan. Hurriedly organizing the Ladies' Hermitage Association, they persuaded the General Assembly to consider selling the entire property to them. Underestimating Tennesseans' devotion to their Confederate soldiers, the women were rebuffed when the Assembly decided to retain 475 acres for construction of a Confederate Home. The *Hermitage* mansion and twenty-five acres went to the Ladies Hermitage Association. For some reason, all of the soldiers were removed from the Confederate Home in 1916 and moved to the Tennessee Industrial School. In 1935, all of the original *Hermitage* property, including the home for Confederate veterans, was transferred to the women operating the *Hermitage*. Failing to grasp the historical significance of the Confederate Soldiers Home, they lost no time in demolishing it. Many of the old soldiers were buried in an attractive circular graveyard under a grove of trees near the old church located on the *Hermitage* property. The cemetery was allowed to remain. (Courtesy Bert Jared)

CHATTANOOGA, TENNESSEE, 1914. James Coleman Oakley was photographed at the UCV Reunion, proudly wearing his reunion badges and ribbons. He had enlisted in the Confederate service on July 3, 1861, in Dickson County, Tennessee. Two years later, he became ill and had to stay behind as the army moved out. Three days later, in attempting to catch up with his regiment, he was captured and sent north to a prison camp. In 1910, while applying for a pension, he learned that he had been listed as a deserter. To a man who even refused to wear blue after the War, saying "not when I suffered so much at the hands of the blue uniform," the charge of desertion stung badly. He wrote a six-page letter to the pension board, recounting his rejection of several attempts to get him to take the Yankee oath. "I told him I could not afford to do it. If there be any honor in being a Confederate soldier I wanted it — if there be any disgrace in being a Confederate soldier I wanted that, too." Records eventually proved he was not a deserter. In 1914, Oakley became ill at the UCV reunion and returned home where he died within a week. (Courtesy Evelyn P'Pool)

MISSISSIPPI, ca 1920. Making a living was tough, but many a family worked a small farm either as tenants or sharecroppers, unless they were lucky enough to own a few acres. The South's strength of character sprang from such people. Honesty was their trademark; faith was their watchword. (Courtesy Elmore Greaves)

ALABAMA, ca. 1861. First Sergeant Elisha B. Dickinson, Co. G, 7th Alabama Infantry, CSA. Sergeant Dickinson, who later served with the 42nd Alabama Infantry, was captured May 23, 1863, at Vicksburg, five days after the siege began. (Courtesy David Hammock)

GADSDEN, ALABAMA, 1926. A gathering of the Emma Sansom Camp No. 275, United Confederate Veterans. The only veteran who can be identified is William F. Kennedy, standing next to the man on the left end. (Courtesy Hunter Phillips)

BIRMINGHAM, ALABAMA, ca. 1880. R.S. Warner, photographed at the Oxford Studio.

DENISON, TEXAS, ca. 1900. Taken in the Moore Studio, this is a picture of Elihu B. Henshaw, president of Bloomfield Seminary. Established by the Methodists in 1852 as Bloomfield Academy, the school for Chickasaw girls was located in the Chickasaw Nation. Denison, a few miles south of the Red River, southern boundary of the Indian Nation, was the nearest Texas city.

PAULS VALLEY, INDIAN TERRITORY, ca. 1898. (Opposite page) In this photograph of Pauls Valley's community band, there stands one lady who made history on November 14, 1899. Miss Anabel Fleming, standing third from the left, was admitted to practice law in the United States Court of the Southern District of Indian Territory, thus becoming the first woman lawyer west of the Mississippi. A remarkably talented lady, she played pump organ at the Methodist church, organized several literary and social clubs, made speeches for the bond drives in World War I, and wrote poetry for several magazines, among them the *Confederate Veteran*. A member of the DAR, she was also active in the Sam Davis Chapter of the UDC. Born January 5, 1874, in Clarksville, Texas, she was twenty-seven years old when she married Charles H. Thomason, a lawyer who had come to Pauls Valley from Paris, Tennessee. From that point, most of her time was spent outside the courtroom and inside her home where she raised the four children born to their marriage. She lived to be seventy-five years old, passing away in her home on September 15, 1949, having made her mark in history a half-century before. In the January, 1900, issue of *Harper's Bazar*, a magazine published in New York and London, her admission to the bar was reported like this:

> The Indian Territory is no longer a reservation. Its latest stride towards full development and probable Statehood is marked by the admission of Miss Anabel Fleming to practise law in the United States court that has jurisdiction over the Chickasaw Nation.
>
> She is a resident of the town of Pauls Valley, and acquired her law knowledge while assisting her father in the court in which she was recently enrolled as a counselor. The town of Pauls Valley, where Miss Fleming resides, is a place of several thousand inhabitants, and there are a score of murder cases pending upon the docket. Upon the day of her admission to the bar Miss Fleming, as her father's assistant, attested the death-warrant of a negro whom Judge Townsend had sentenced to be hanged on January 13, 1900.
>
> Miss Fleming, however, despite her association with the bloody justice of the frontier, is a young lady of highly cultivated manner, and though her legal attainments were only known to her intimate friends, her preeminent social and intellectual qualities have been recognized by all who know her. She is distinctly the leader of society in her community, and is thoroughly conventional. She is Southern born and Southern bred, of Scotch ancestry, and her family is among the best known and best connected in the State of Texas. . . . Her grandfather, Hon. W.H. Fleming, commanded a regiment in the Confederate service. . . . Titus County, Texas, was named for Miss Fleming's maternal grandfather.
>
> Miss Fleming's lineage is from the family stock that settled in Wilmington, Delaware, in the seventeenth century, and held its reunion at Fairmount, West virginia, in 1891, with thousands of representatives, including the Governors of West Virginia and Florida.

(Courtesy Adrienne Grimmett)

TENNESSEE, ca. 1903. This may be
a scene on the Cumberland River,
possibly the landing at Nashville.
The upper decks are crowded with
passengers; the lower one holds
cargo. (Courtesy Edwin P'Pool)

NASHVILLE, TENNESSEE, ca.
1890s. (Opposite page) Steamboats
docked on the Cumberland River.
In the upper photo, the second
boat can be identified as the *J.B.
Richards*. Below, the first boat is the
*Abigail*, and the third one is the
*Bob Dudley*. (Courtesy Edwin
P'Pool)

NORTH CAROLINA, ca. 1913.
Cutting cane for sorghum molasses. The cane is cooked in flat,
open-air vats. Skimmed and stirred
continuously, it cooks down into a
thick, dark syrup called molasses.

DUCK HILL, MISSISSIPPI, August 21, 1861. Made when he enlisted, this picture shows a 21-year-old Mississippian ready to defend his state. Robert Gray, born May 25, 1840, in Lodi, Mississippi, joined Company B, 15th Mississippi Infantry, and served the Confederacy until his unit was surrendered at Durham Station, North Carolina, in April, 1865. On the opposite page, Gray is shown with his daughter, Exesah, in a studio portrait made at Wesson, Miss., in 1890, and with his son, John, in a snapshot made at Columbus, Miss., on November 2, 1916. The occasion for the latter photograph was a UCV reunion. Here, the venerated old veteran proudly wears his reunion badge and Southern Cross of Honor. Six months later, Robert Gray passed away and was buried at Salem Church in Salem, Mississippi. (Courtesy Robert W. Betterton, Jr.)

LOUISIANA, ca. 1912. Stopping for a rest by the side of the road.

ST. SIMON'S ISLAND, GEORGIA, ca. 1930. (Opposite page) This moss-draped road looks much like many an old road in south Georgia and north Florida.

NEW ORLEANS, LOUISIANA, 1890s. Interior views of private homes of the period are somewhat rare. The photographs below and on the opposite page were made by C. Milo Williams.

ARDMORE, OKLAHOMA. (Opposite page) Built in 1910, the old Confederate Home and its dependencies, which are not shown in these pictures, are still standing. When the last Confederate soldier passed away in the 1940s, the facilities were given to the state of Oklahoma to house Oklahoma veterans of subsequent wars. No structural changes have been made, and the home's exterior remains as it appears here. The picture at the top of the page was taken during a workday in 1912. The lower photograph, showing a newly arrived load of watermelons, was made in 1914. (Courtesy Ardmore Public Library)

CULLMAN, ALABAMA, ca. 1907. A young men's Sunday School class at the Methodist Church. Sim Lovelady, probably the teacher, stands on the back row holding an ornate, fringed banner which reads: BANNER CLASS. Only two of the boys can be identified. Paul Cook is seated second from the left end of the second row, and Charlie Sandlin is second from the right end of the same row. Many a southern boy learned the principles of faith, honor, and good citizenship in church classes such as this.

RICHMOND, VIRGINIA, 1938. (Opposite page) This, the most magnificent of our Confederate monuments, began as a dream in the minds of the old soldiers. By 1899, the United Confederate Veterans had raised $20,000 — a princely sum in those poor days in Dixie — towards the building of a permanent tribute to President Davis. Turning it over to the United Daughters of the Confederacy, they requested help from the ladies in completing the project. With the end in sight and most of the $70,000 raised, the old veterans chose Richmond for their 1907 reunion and dedication of the Jefferson Davis Monument. All eyes turned to Richmond. Listen to the description of that momentous occasion.

> On June 3, 1907 . . . the great monument was unveiled with all the pomp and pageantry that could be commanded in the city of Richmond. It was a wonderfully inspiring occasion — a sea of faces in every direction . . . faces of thousands of Confederate veterans, of thousands and tens of thousands of men and women who had come from near and far to do homage to their beloved chieftain, and who had brought their children to be a part of the unforgettable occasion. . .
>
> How inspiring were the addresses, Mrs. Holmes presenting the monument to Mrs. Henderson for the United Daughters of the Confederacy, and Senator E.W. Carmack, Tennessee, making the principal address! How wonderful the parade — U.C.V. officials on horseback leading, followed by carriages filled with officers of the Confederated Southern Memorial Association, general officers of the U.D.C., and Division presidents, and how many, many veterans in Confederate gray were in the parade, and the famous Richmond Blues and Howitzers in full uniform!
>
> The canvas was pulled aside by Margaret Howell Davis Hayes, only living child of Jefferson Davis, and her young son, Jefferson Hayes-Davis. Then there was boom of cannon firing the salute, and small Confederate flags shot from their mouths and settled down over the crowd, to be seized by eager hands for souvenirs.

The Jefferson Davis Monument is the centerpiece of Monument Avenue, often called the most beautiful street in America. The bricked streets are divided by a central grassy median which runs the entire length of Monument Avenue. At every intersection, there is an enormous statue of a Confederate hero — five of them in all. Jeb Stuart, Matthew Fontaine Maury, Stonewall Jackson, Robert E. Lee, and Davis. The entire scene is surrounded by an unbroken stretch of Victorian row houses, virtually unchanged from their original appearance, and is reminiscent of European landscape and statuary. It is truly the pride of the entire South.

Today, all of the monuments are in danger. The black city council and mayor of Richmond have announced a diabolical scheme to denigrate the memory of our fallen heroes by placing next to each statue a modern sculpture of a negro, from banjo players to abolitionists to civil rights activists. First plans called for removal and destruction of the monuments, but further deliberation produced the idea that perversion of the monuments would more effectively insult the white population of the South.

ARLINGTON, VIRGINIA, ca. 1915. The monument to the Confederate dead in Arlington National Cemetery. Built primarily with funds from the UDC, it was unveiled on June 4, 1914, although the seed-thought of this monument was sown in 1898 when President McKinley suggested in an Atlanta speech that it was time that the north share with the South in the care of Confederate graves. Until then, no Confederate soldiers were allowed burial in the National Cemetery. Eventually, a Confederate section was designated and permission given for the bodies of 267 Confederate soldiers buried in and near the city of Washington to be sought out and re-interred in this Confederate section. In sharp contrast, it is sad to note the bigotry and intolerance that now attend each year's Memorial Day ceremonies. Upon nearly every occasion, the military band refuses to play "Dixie," Confederate flags are banned, and several U.S. Senators *from our own region* ignore the affair, refusing to send memorial wreaths representing their respective southern states.

LOUISIANA, ca. 1880s. The South had it all. Magnolias, Spanish moss, southern belles, southern drawls — and steamboats! Here, the luxurious *John W. Cannon* is docked somewhere on the Mississippi River. Steamboats added a truly romantic element to what was becoming an almost legendary bit of phraseology — *the southern way of life.*

BROOKHAVEN, MISSISSIPPI, ca. 1915. Z.Z. Turnbough's Horse Palace. (Courtesy Elmore Greaves)

BEAUFORT, SOUTH CAROLINA, ca. 1930s. (Opposite page) Built before the Revolutionary War by William Elliott, *The Anchorage* is one of the loveliest homes in the low country of South Carolina.

MISSISSIPPI, ca. 1890. (Opposite page) This woman and her two sons pose for a traveling photographer in front of their rural Mississippi home. Although it is barely visible in this picture, there is an open breezeway running through the center of this house, dividing the house into two separate sections. A common style of architecture in the 19th-century South, these homes were located primarily in rural areas, and the breezeways were often referred to as dogtrots. (Courtesy Elmore Greaves)

ASHVILLE, ALABAMA, 1923. Gathered for a photograph in front of the Confederate statue at the St. Clair County Courthouse are several old veterans and their UDC sponsors. Lt. Colonel John Inzer, of the 58th Alabama Infantry, is the seventh man from the right end of the second row. Highest ranking officer of St. Clair County, he was the last survivor of those who signed the Alabama Act of Secession in 1861. (Courtesy Hunter Phillips)

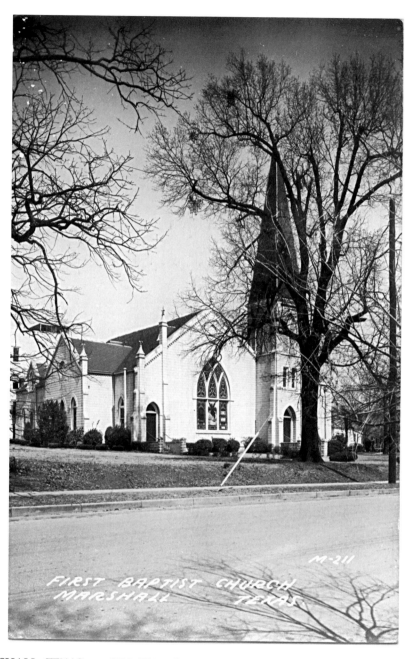

MARSHALL, TEXAS, ca. 1939. This photograph was enlarged from a postcard to emphasize the beauty of this building, the First Baptist Church. Although the card was mailed in 1948, the photograph was probably taken about 1939, and the church was built much earlier than that. J.H. Sayles, a minister, was probably holding a two-week revival at the church when he wrote to another minister, M.M. Fulmer, in Uvalde, Texas. "We arrived safe. We are having a fine meeting. The Lord blessed us with one candidate for baptism last night."

NEW ORLEANS, LOUISIANA, April, 1923. When the United Confederate Veterans met for their annual reunion, it was the fifth time New Orleans had hosted the event. Even though the gray ranks were growing mighty thin, the old veterans still exhibited a remarkable amount of spunk. In a stormy session, the membership rejected a suggestion that all future reunions be held in conjunction with Union veterans' organizations, denounced northern interlopers who charged that the South had rebelled against the government, refused to increase their diminishing ranks by accepting sons and daughters into the actual membership, and tried to determine how best to stop the "teaching of false history in Southern schools." When it began to rain at the outset of their parade, a reporter asked one old soldier who carried the Confederate flag if he wasn't afraid of getting wet. "Rain's not botherin' us," he replied. "We're all too well seasoned to get warped."

NEW ORLEANS, LOUISIANA, April, 1923. (Next pages) Both of these photographs were made at the reunion of the United Confederate Veterans. In the second picture, the old soldier on the left is from the Lomax Camp in Montgomery, Alabama. (Courtesy Edwin P'Pool)

A. — APRIL 1923. SOUTHERN FOTO FILM NEWS SERVICE

CLEMSON, SOUTH CAROLINA, ca. 1930s. (Opposite page) *Fort Hill*, its name derived from the site having once been fortified against Indian attack, is one of the most important antebellum homes in the South, for it was the home of the South's preeminent statesman of the first half of the nineteenth century, John Caldwell Calhoun. He served as secretary of war under President Monroe, vice-president under Presidents John Quincy Adams and Andrew Jackson, secretary of state under President Tyler, and U.S. senator from South Carolina, a position he held until his death March 31, 1850. The undisputed champion of states' rights, he defined and made practical application of that great constitutional principle, a cherished doctrine of lovers of freedom the world over and one that would guide the South in her quest for independence during the 1860s as well as her defense against the forced integration of the 1960s. On March 4, 1850, Calhoun was too ill to deliver his final speech in the U.S. Senate, having instead to sit and listen as Senator Mason read the remarks in defense of southern rights. In Calhoun's last piece of correspondence, he wrote that it was "difficult to see how two peoples so different and hostile can exist together in one common Union." Showing a keen sense of what was to come, his last spoken words fairly predicted the events of the 1860s. "The South, the poor South."

CHARLOTTE, NORTH CAROLINA, ca. 1903. The Carnegie Library served the citizens of Charlotte from 1903 until it was demolished in 1956. *Demolished*. The word reads like an epitaph to the architecture of the South. In the South's rush to remake itself in the image of the north, its architectural elegance — like its very soul — has given way to tawdry examples of glass and steel and cement blocks shaped at their very best into square, gray, cracker-box creations that both embarrass and blight the southern landscape.

STONE MOUNTAIN, GEORGIA, ca. 1916. Stone Mountain, the largest body of solid granite in the world, is seen in this postcard view before the work began on the giant carving of Davis, Jackson, and Lee.

STATESVILLE, NORTH CAROLINA, July 12, 1939. Published by Rose's 5-10-25¢ Stores, this postcard features the Iredell County Court House and monument to Confederate soldiers. North Carolinians were justly proud of their men in gray, for North Carolina furnished more soldiers to the Confederacy than any other state.

ATLANTA, GEORGIA, July 20, 1925. (Opposite page) When the South was southern, so were its governors. At the Southern Governors' Conference, these men took charge of the sale of the South's share of the Confederate memorial half dollars, the proceeds of which were used to finance the carving on Stone Mountain. On the front row, from left to right, are Hollis N. Randolph, president of Stone Mountain Confederate Monumental Association; Gov. John W. Martin, of Florida; Gov. Thomas G. McLeod, of South Carolina; Gov. W.W. Brandon, of Alabama; Gov. Henry L. Whitfield, of Mississippi; A.B. Foster, representing Gov. Miriam A. Ferguson, of Texas; Robert F. Maddox and G.F. Willis of the Memorial Association.

On the back row, are Fons Hathway, Secretary to Gov. Martin; A.S. Caldwell, representing Gov. Austin Peay, of Tennessee; Eugene R. Black of the Memorial Association; Lt. Gov. H.H. Denhardt, of Kentucky; Gen. R.A. Snead, representing Gov. M.E. Trapp, of Oklahoma; Gen. W.B. Freeman, Commander-in-Chief, UCV, representing Gov. E. Lee Trinkle, of Virginia; James J. Bailey, representing Gov. Henry L. Fuqua, of Louisiana; Col. W.L. Peel of the Memorial Association.

# Acknowledgement

In thanking those who lend aid to such an endeavor as this, one runs the embarrassing risk of overlooking someone, but that hazard alone cannot excuse the recipient of such invaluable assistance for failing to try to enumerate those within his memory.

First and foremost among my generous supporters are the two most important people in my life, my mother and my daddy. Without their constant support, encouragement, and input, much of the flavor of this nostalgic effort would be missing, and hard would have been the task of completing the whole project. My brother, Patrick, has been of immediate service and general support throughout.

The Word Mill, typesetters and photo specialists for this project, went above and beyond the call of duty in executing their duties. Al Thomas, who has set the type on all three of my books, exhibited the patience of Job as he labored to meet every one of my detailed specifications.

Two others deserve special mention. Hunter Phillips came to my rescue with splendid photographs of Confederate soldiers and those all-important re-unions, supplying every copy at his own expense. Edwin P'Pool, also at his own expense, opened his extensive private collection to me at no charge whatsoever.

In addition, I wish to thank the following people for their contributions: Jenanne Verrell, Bob Blackburn, Ruth Gammill, James Cochran, Guy William Logsdon, Emita Whicker, J.L. Day, Ruby Ozment, Irene Whited, Jim Yarbrough, Phillip Jackson, Dave Tolley, Gordon Pickrell, Darlene Trent, Larry Alderman, Ginger Turner, Verna Dell Tolson, James David Altman, David Workman, Henry Googer, Adrienne Grimmett, Elmore Greaves, Louise Niedermaier, Leta Rae McClain, Leta Ferguson, James Turner, Pete Mitchell, Elwood Morris, Evelyn P'Pool, Ken P'Pool, Butch Moxley, Lynn Moxley, Stephen Carter, Bert Jared, Manie Whitmeyer, William F. King, Anne Armour, Helen Crawford, David Hammock, Julie Prim, Haywood Vaughan, Scott Bradford, Bobby Mitchell, Bob Betterton, Ben Grimland, Ann Clements, Ron Bryant, Paul Mott, Miriam Brown, Sheryl Jaggers, Sally Ray, Bill Warren, Robert Sapp. Carol Ann Aby, Carol Tenpenny, Ouida Jones, Leona Holland, Ben Crump, Betty Wright, Scott Smith, Juanita Tate, and Mark Chastain.

Also, Mr. & Mrs. Johnny Herbert, Mr. & Mrs. L.L. Shirley, Mr. & Mrs. Port Schnorrenberg, and Mr. & Mrs. Albert Baxendale, Jr.

# Index

Brandon, W.W., 371
Brinkley, Ark., 12
Brenau College, 119
Brewton, Ala., 133
Brockenbrough, John, 243
Brookhaven, Miss., 361
Brooks, H., 148
Brown, John C., 63
Brown, Joseph Emerson, 308
Brown, Mrs. John C., 63
Brown, Miriam, 341
Brownsville, Texas, 113
Buchanan, J.A., 233
Buck, Silas C., 335
Buckner, Simon Bolivar, 271
Burkes, Andrew Jackson, 39, 87, 327-328
Burkes, Cecil Hope, 87
Burkes, Eulalie, 87, 91, 327
Burkes, Edna, 91
Burkes, Queenie Verlie, 87
Burkes, Vida, 35
Burkes, William Hilliard, 4, 39, 327
Burkhalter, Edwina, 268
Burks, John, 95
Burks, Rowena, 95
Burks, W.S., 78
Burnett, Frances Hodgson, 292
Burwell, Mrs., 267
Bushyhead, I.T., 289
Butler, Benjamin F., 306

Cabell, W.L., 63
Caddo, Indian Territory, 30
Calcasieu Parish, La., 231
Caldwell, A.S., 371
Calhoun, John C., 137, 369
Cameron, Mrs., 312
Carmack, Edward Ward, 42, 359
Carmichael, Mary, 263
Carr, Bonnie, 126, 267
Carroll, Ance, 273
Carroll County, Va., 5, 47, 55
Carter, Beulah Mae, 273
Carter, Fanny, 273
Carter, James Marion, 273
Carter, Stephen L., 273
Cartledge, Rhoda, 321
Cathey, George L., 92
Charleston, S.C., 116, 137, 153, 185, 208, 222-223, 241
Charlotte, N.C., 106, 369
Charlottesville, Va., 175
Chase, William Merritt, 67

Chattanooga, Tenn., 61, 93, 139, 145, 161, 165, 181, 237, 345
Cherokee Indians, 39, 69, 111
Chickasaw Indians, 111, 304, 348
Choctaw Indians, 111
Clark, Kate Freeman, 67
Clarksdale, Miss., 218
Clarksville, Texas, 349
Claybrooke, Misses, 201
Cleburne, Pat, 342
Cleburne, Texas, 27, 97
Clemson, S.C., 369
Cline, W.M., 145
Cochran, Eula, 267
Cochran, Frank, 303
Cochran, Pierce, 267
Cock, Lewis, 267
Cock, Will, 267
Coleman, Gov., 245
Coleman, Will, 67
College Park, Ga., 31, 201
Columbia, S.C., 294, 306-307, 309, 318-320
Columbus, Ga., 135, 147
Columbus, Miss., 107, 352
Combs, Edna, 336
Combs, Kathleen, 336
Confederate monuments, 104-105, 138-139, 151, 153, 157, 161, 165, 168, 183, 193, 199, 201, 206, 209, 213, 219, 221, 227, 231, 241, 243, 245, 247, 254, 358, 360, 363
Confederate soldiers, 5, 10, 17, 19, 28, 31, 46, 50, 56-58, 65, 68, 72-73, 76, 78, 83, 88-89, 92, 100-101, 103-105, 122, 178, 262, 276-277, 334, 336, 340-342, 345-347, 352-353, 363, 365-367
Confederate Soldier' Homes, 5, 152, 178, 248, 342, 344, 356
Confederate Veteran (magazine), 2, 8, 46, 58, 92, 103, 114, 277, 296, 349
Conway, Ark., 192
Cook, Mrs. D.C., 115
Cook, Paul, 357
Cooke County, Texas, 168
Cooley, Theodore, 71
Cooper, Minnie, 304
Cooper, Texas, 288
Corinth, Miss., 71, 125
Corpus Christi, Texas, 230
Cottage Gardens (house), 187
cotton, 2, 7, 23, 140, 156, 163, 170-171, 242, 255
Counce, Wirt, 125
Courtney, E.L., 51

376

*Sutherland* (house), 184

Tallahassee, Fla., 207
Tallassee, Ala., 77
Tampa, Fla., 257
Taylor, Emma, 267
Taylor, Miss, 267
Taylor, Myrtle, 97
Taylor, Zachary, 328
Telephone, Texas, 4, 327
Tennessee, 3, 5, 42, 63, 81, 91, 145, 291, 294, 329, 351, 371
*Tennessee Belle* (steamboat), 23
Tenpenny, Carol, 102
Texarkana, Ark., 225, 233
Texas, 26, 63, 75, 91, 156, 268, 280, 299, 330, 371
Thelma _____, 187
Thomason, Charles H., 349
Thomasville, Ga., 150
Thompson, C.A., 71
Thompson, Clifton, 100
Thompson, Clinton C., 49, 100
Thompson, Estella, 91
Thompson, Grace, 100
Thompson, Ira, 100
Thompson, James M., 49, 100
Thompson, Mattie, 173
Thompson, Oscar, 327
Thompson, Roy, 100
Thompson, Ruth, 100
Thompson's Station, Tenn., 71
Thonotosassa, Fla., 49
*Three Oaks* (house), 188
Thuss, A.J., 54
Thuss, W.G., 54
Timrod, Henry, 241
Tioga, Texas, 111
Titus County, Texas, 349
Todd County, Ky., 151
Tolbert, George, 22
Tolbert, Jack, 22
Toney, M.B., 71
Townsend, Judge, 349
Trapp, M.E., 371
Trent, Darlene, 49
Trinkle, E. Lee, 371
Tullahoma, Tenn., 98, 264
Tullis, Miss Watson, 240
Tulsa, Indian Territory, 7, 185
Turnbough, Z.Z., 361
Turner, J.M., 71
Turner, James K., 336

Tuscaloosa, Ala., 342
Tuscumbia, Ala., 335
Twain, Mark, 249
Tyler, John, 37, 369
Tyler, Texas, 84-85
Tyne, W.A., 288

Uncle John, 319-320
United Confederate Veterans, 31, 55, 68, 87, 103, 165, 263, 296, 335-336, 341, 345, 352, 359, 365, 371
United Daughters of the Confederacy, 5, 46, 55, 62-63, 68, 71, 87, 116, 126, 185, 201, 277, 296, 331, 339, 345, 349, 359-360, 363
University of Central Arkansas, 192
University of Chattanooga, 181
University of Richmond, 190
University of the South, 271, 341
Upshur County, Texas, 103
Uvalde, Texas, 364

Van Hoose, Jennie, 296
Vance, Zebulon, 138
Vanderbilt, George W., 216
Venable, Richard M., 271
Vicksburg, Miss., 2, 23, 213
Virginia, 50, 63, 127, 274, 338, 371
Virginia Military Institute, 311

Walker, Rachel, 212
Wallace, George, 37
Walner, Acca, 267
Walner, Julia, 267
Walnut Ridge, Ark., 144
Warner, R.S., 347
Washington and Lee University, 83
Washington, D.C., 127, 179, 360
Washington, George, 83, 267
Washington, Martha, 267
Watertown, Tenn., 141
Watie, Stand, 69
Weatherford, Texas, 75, 206
Webb, Mrs. L.D., 240
Webster, Maud, 148
Weed, Mrs. Edwin, 63
Wesson, Miss., 352
West, Mae, 267
West Point, Miss., 71
Westmoreland, Va., 250
Wetumka, Okla., 35, 39, 91, 108, 255, 327-328